MW00613103

THE FOUR PRINCIPLES

*Applying the Four Keys of
Authentic Acting to Life*

On E. Katherine Kerr and The Four Principles

"*The Four Principles* book is not the usual 'how-to'—this is the kind of inspirational, passed on knowledge, that I don't believe has ever been put in a book before. Invaluable."

—June Havoc, actress, author, director

"I stayed up to eight A.M. reading your book. It kept reassuring me that I'm not crazy—that it's okay to feel despair. It also made me think I don't care if I am crazy. I want so many people to read it."

—Lisa Rock, stand-up comedian, actress

"My husband doesn't like to read much, but he saw something good happening to me and asked me what was going on. I gave him your book to read. He called me from El Paso the other night at two A.M. to tell me how much he liked it. Thanks a lot."

—Sheri Andrews, actress

"I've turned so many people on to your book. I read it again last week! It has done wonders for me in so many areas of my life. Thanks!"

—Christina Malpero

"I am not being facetious when I write that E. Katherine Kerr's manuscript is one of the most important works on acting I have ever felt compelled to turn down. It is an extraordinary meditation on the nature of being and acting. The actor who resists the life force that pulsates through Kerr's work wears more than a mask; he has been overtaken and captured by a suit of armor that ironically only someone of Kerr's savvy hard-ass mystical talents might strip away. And if it were actually and purely about acting, I would do more than admire the text and its author...her audience, to my mind may not be about actors at all, but any constructively bewildered member of the public who finds himself on a quest for self. Rest assured I will buy fifty copies right off the presses for our shop and will personally advocate it at every opportunity."

—Glenn Young, president, Applause Books

"If I'd had you and your class when I was out there in the world of show business, I wouldn't have gotten mangled the way I did."

—Liz McDonald, actress, playwright

"I was having a very difficult time getting pregnant. I reread your book. My husband and I went to France, and I applied your techniques! Matthew Charles was born July 17, 1997!"

—Gina Carillo, stand-up comedian, actress

"I've known Katherine since 1981 when I saw her perform Off Broadway in Caryl Churchill's play *Cloud 9*. I was so excited and moved by her performance (and by the play) that I saw the production three times. In 1987 as I was writing my play *Laughing Wild*, which has a very demanding leading female role, I began to picture Katherine in the part. And she and I then acted together in the play's premiere Off Broadway at Playwrights Horizons.

Katherine began *The Creative Explosion* workshop which I did. It was an emotionally and professional rich workshop, and also one of great bonding among the participants. I am always running into young actors who, upon realizing I know Katherine, tell me with enormous enthusiasm how much they have benefited from her classes. Sometimes they feel their lives have been changed. She brings a sharp intelligence, her own acting abilities (which are substantial), her desire to help and empower people, her sense of humor, her sense of play, a gift for helping people work through artistic and personal blocks, and her inability to settle when she can imagine something better."

—*Christopher Durang, Tony Award-winning playwright*

"I want you to know how much your class helped me in my job. I gave a presentation to 150 travel agents the other evening, and it was so much fun! I used your special skills that you taught us and was comfortable—present and really with my audience. I even walked around with the mike, instead of standing behind the podium. I was very relaxed, and one of my customers sent me an email asking if I ever thought of being a motivational speaker! I learned so much from you—I am forever grateful!"

—*Gail Goldberg, speaker, travel agent*

"I want to thank you again for *The Creative Explosion* workshop. An unforgettable weekend! What I have been left with is indescribable. It feels like a precious jewel in the centre of my heart. What a gift you have for touching the core of the spirit in everything you do and are. It will sustain me."

—*Carol Lynn Reifel, professor, Queens University, Ontario, Canada*

"Wow! Your inspiration is more than helpful. It's inspiring. It's daring. It's brave. NEVER have I EVER been so willing to let go and have faith, be courageous, daring, open, giving, and willing to share myself, until I started on this journey. It's so deep. You have opened up my eyes not only as a performer, but as a writer, as a person. You've exposed me to me. And overall, I feel whole again. You've brought me back to the beginning...to a place I once was a very long time ago when I was young."

—*Richard Luciano, actor, writer*

THE FOUR PRINCIPLES

Applying the Four Keys of
Authentic Acting to Life

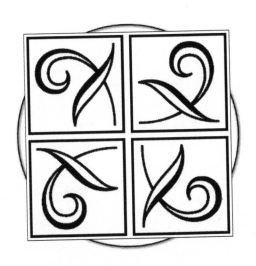

E. KATHERINE KERR

Copyright © 1993, 2008, 2010, 2011-2015 by E. Katherine Kerr

ISBN: 978-0-9895493-0-1 Softcover

All rights reserved. No part of this book may be reproduced or transmitted in any form or by any means, electronic or mechanical, including photocopying, recording or by any information storage or retrieval system, without permission from the copyright owner.

Copyright © 2010 under the title *The Four Principles: Applying the Keys of Brilliant Acting to Life*

Copyright © 2008 under the title *All the World's a Stage: Applying the Principles of Brilliant Acting to Brilliant Living*

Copyright © 1993 as an unpublished work

The author's note to *the dreamer examines his pillow*, Copyright © 1987 by John Patrick Shanley. All rights reserved. Quotation used by permission of the author.

Project development: Martha Rhodes, mrgraphicdetails@aol.com

Book cover: Elizabeth Pasternack, epasternackdesign@gmail.com

Line editor and interior design: Jeffrey Polsky, jeffrey@jeffreypolsky.com

Additional copies of *The Four Principles* may be ordered at TheFourPrinciples.com or Amazon.com.

In the third scene of this play, Dad says, "The individual life is a dream." For me, personally, this is a most moving idea. It frees me from my fear of death. It puts my ego where it belongs, in a place of secondary importance. It binds me to the human race, and binds the race itself to the atoms in the stars.

Who am I? This is a courageous question. As a writer and as a man I am involved in one central struggle—to discover and accept who I am. I believe all fear has its roots in denial. I have, at one time or another, denied everything. Every fact of my specific self. My parents, my Bronx origin, my Americanness, my Irishness, my appetites, my mortality, my need for love and acceptance, my jealousy, my violence, my anger.

I am not a courageous person by nature. I have simply discovered that, at certain key moments in this life, you must find courage in yourself, in order to move forward and live. It is like a muscle and it must be exercised, first a little, and then more and more. All the really exciting things possible during the course of a lifetime require a little more courage than we currently have. A deep breath and a leap.

Writing is acting is directing is living your life. I have told you the things I have just told you so that you know something of my approach to playwriting. I see no difference between writing a play and living my life. The same things that make a moment in my life succeed, combust, move, these same things make a moment in my playwriting have life. And when I move in my writing, I have moved in my life. There is no illusion. It is all the same thing.

Acting is the same as playwriting.

—John Patrick Shanley,
Author's Note to his play *the dreamer examines his pillow*

CONTENTS

INTRODUCTION

If I could, I would write this book on a ball. None of The Four Principles would be first, and all of them would be first—and last. The ball would have no top, no bottom, no beginning, no middle, and no end.

In fact, these Four Principles are not complete unless they are together. They work synergistically. You can't know what you're truly committed to until you are present, but you can't be present unless you are willing (Relaxation), and you can't move along your path without Communication. And as soon as you commit to something, the barriers begin to pop up, so you have to Be Present to get past them—on and on around the ball, turning it over and over, rolling with it through life. You must continue to apply The Four Principles to keep the ball moving. And that's what this whole book is about: creating movement—movement along the path toward your heart's desires, movement toward your realization as a human being.

I considered putting the book on a spiral binding with four different covers, so that you, the reader, could start anywhere. Each principle would be the beginning or the end of the book. I wrote this version with that in mind. However, it was too complicated logistically, not to mention expensive. I have to present it in a linear form, so I chose to begin with the principle of Being Present. For me personally, this is where I must begin, but you may open the book to any principle you choose: Commitment, Communication, Relaxation, or Being Present. It is up to you.

In the original version, many rewrites and many years ago, I began the book with Commitment. At the time the book was called *The Creative Explosion: A Simple Guide to Brilliant Acting.* I thought I was writing a book about acting, but it wanted to be something else. I resisted it the way artists sometimes do with their creations or parents do with their children. Finally, I relented and let the book be what it wanted to be: how The Four Principles apply to life.

Although the purpose of the book changed, what never changed are The Four Principles. They are the same. They have been the same since they appeared to me many years ago. The change has been in my understanding, respect, and experience of them.

The Four Principles came to me through an odd doorway perhaps, through acting and through teaching acting to others. It is an unusual path to enlightenment, but the Universe will use anything to wake us up. We all have our own paths. Diverse as they may be, I believe these Four Principles apply to them all.

As John Patrick Shanley wrote in his author's note to *the dreamer examines his pillow*, "Writing is acting is directing is living your life....I see no difference between writing a play and living my life. The same things that make a moment in my life succeed, combust, move, these same things make a moment in my playwriting have life. And when I move in my writing, I have moved in my life. There is no illusion. It is all the same thing. Acting is the same as playwriting."

Being an actor is difficult because our bodies and who we are as people are all we have. We have no instruments or particular skills to fall back on—nothing but ourselves. On the one hand, we must be able to be both completely open and vulnerable; and on the other, have thick enough skin to withstand the slings and arrows of outrageous rejections and criticism. We have to learn a great deal about self-mastery.

Many of us become actors because of an unexpressed yearning for the love we never got as children. When we mature, we learn that the greatest satisfaction comes when we express our love and light, rather than try to get the love we never had.

Along the way there are all sorts of hidden traps and demons. It is a life of extremes: feast and famine, success and failure, riches and bankruptcy. If we fail at self-mastery, we can fall into addictions and step onto the low road to hell. The people who succeed in becoming self-aware and self-responsible, not necessarily in becoming stars, lead truly fulfilling lives.

It was my students who began telling me that The Four Principles were affecting not only their acting but also their lives. As a natural outgrowth, I developed a two-day workshop called *The*

Creative Explosion. The purpose of the workshop is *to release the energy to start on the path to your heart's desires and keep going.* It is about movement and self-empowerment. I have conducted four or five of those workshops every year over the last twenty-five years.

I am not a guru, and I do not believe in assuming some god-like stance. In fact, watching the downfall of certain gurus and powerful spiritual leaders has taught me how dangerous that is. I jokingly refer to myself as a *felicitator.* I do my best to maintain humility and an eye-level relationship with my students. I am human. I have lots of cracks and crevices and wounded places. Therefore, in this book I express these Four Principles in a very personal way. I am continuing to grow and expand through The Four Principles myself. I am not *there* yet. In fact, there is no *there* to get to—only surprising new levels and places.

I have watched as The Four Principles help people open to a creative energy that is larger than they are and challenges them to expand no matter what career they have chosen. This creative force uses our unique talents and personalities to heal and enlighten; it makes us laugh, feel, and open our hearts. It connects us with one another. It relieves our pain and fear and teaches us to experience joy and ecstasy. When we can use that energy and let it use us, it is a powerful, spiritual experience. This creative force is what we desire in our hearts. Yet, because it is so powerful, it often terrifies us. The Four Principles help us to get through the terror.

Empowerment and spiritual enrichment are why I am so committed to creativity. The act of creating is like casting a new vision of ourselves into the future. Once it is created, we must grow up to it in order to take care of it. We create a child, and we must grow up ourselves in order to take care of it. We can turn away. We can reject it, but it is there forever. It may take years to allow, embrace, and empower our creations, but it is worth the time and effort. Artists must empower themselves in order to take care of their own creations. Our creations are our teachers.

Some months after I thought I had finished this book (it still does not feel finished), I was in a ten-minute silence at the beginning of a *Creative Explosion* workshop. It was a lovely, warm October morning. I was sitting on my deck looking out at the woods. The word *Mystery* popped into my mind. "It is another chapter in the book," I heard. It startled me.

"Does that mean that Mystery is a fifth principle?" I wondered wide-eyed.

"No," came the answer clearly and distinctly. "Mystery is not a fifth principle. Mystery is what is at the center of all the principles. It is what surrounds them all. It is what connects them. It is what one experiences when one fully realizes any of The Four Principles."

I sometimes think this book will never be finished. It will certainly never be perfect. Someone may just have to rip it out of my hands. Or, I may just have to let go. It may be difficult, because each version has put me through my paces and stretched me. I have resisted the book, yet it insists on being. I have judged myself for hubris, yet The Four Principles constantly remind me that they are a gift to be received by those who want and need them. My heart-felt wish is that my communication of these Four Principles is good enough to do them justice and help the readers along their path.

E. Katherine Kerr
January 2015

BEING PRESENT

Sensation is at the heart of acting.
—Simon Callow

I am tempted to declare, "Being Present really is the first principle! *This* is the beginning of the book! If you could just Be Present, all else would fall into place! It is the most important principle!"

In Simon Callow's autobiography he wrote about his hard lesson learning how to *be* in acting. In *Flying Blind* he wrote of his failures in his work until one night when he accidentally cracked his head on a beam just as he was going on stage. He was so dazed that he couldn't control himself: all he could be was dazed. For the first time that night his performance worked. He said that he had not been capable of simply being there until this accident.

Authentic acting has about it a sense of immediacy—an electricity. Great actors have *presence*. It is the same in life. The more present we are, the more alive, the more competent, and the clearer our thinking will be. People in my classes who are present often express great joy after performing. It is like being in what athletes call The Zone. Highly skilled athletes experience it as they ski down hill or get a ball to a goal line. A shift in weight or not being aware of the tackler can make the difference between winning and losing, which in downhill racing or football is sometimes measured in milliseconds and inches. Often the greatest task athletes or performers have is to get out of their own way and not think too much. Learning how to Be Present in the body allows one to react quickly and instinctively in the moment.

There is the old joke about a man asking a farmer for directions to town, and the farmer replies, "Sorry. You can't get there from here." The truth is, in life you can't get there *unless* you are here: unless you know where you are, you cannot get to where you want to go. In fact, you won't even know where you want to go if you are expending your energy trying not to be *here*. You must Be Present in order to know what you want. And when you go for what you want, you must Be Present. *The greater your Commitment and the greater your obstacles, the more you need to Be Present.* This is how Commitment and Being Present dance together.

You may not know exactly what it is to Be Present, but you can certainly spot it in others. It is sometimes called charisma. Great actors, athletes, politicians, powerful people, and performers have it whether they are conscious of it or not. Fortunately, one does not have to be born with it. It is something that can be developed consciously.

CLOUD 9

I learned what it means to Be Present during the run of Caryl Churchill's *Cloud 9* Off Broadway. I had worked on moment-to-moment acting and being real on stage in my career, but I had a whopping lesson coming to me after we opened the play. I had been privileged to speak a beautifully written monologue about learning self-love. I identified with it. It meant a great deal to me. I was always moved to tears by it. During rehearsal, the director, Tommy Tune, kept placing the monologue later and later in the play. Finally, he put it right at the end. Opening night went very well. Almost every review favorably mentioned the monologue and my performance of it.

It was a monologue in which I simply sat on a chair and spoke directly to the audience. The light spilling off the stage illuminated most of the audience, so I could clearly see their reactions. I loved the rapt faces, the tears coursing down cheeks, the snapping of purses as women reached for tissues, and the men shifting and reaching into their pockets for their own handkerchiefs. People in the audience sought me out afterward to tell me how much the monologue affected them and changed their lives, and how they hadn't understood the play until my monologue. A woman came up to me in the post office in Wilton, burst into tears, and thanked me. Somehow that monologue had helped her heal her relationship with her brother.

The pressure built. I felt an enormous responsibility toward the monologue, and I was scared. I dried up. With each performance I was feeling less and less. Seeing the audience as well as I could, I noticed that they were no longer moved either. Every performance got worse. Unaware that I could see them, the audience demonstrated clear signs of boredom. Pocketbooks no longer snapped open. And horror of horrors, people were actually reading their programs while I was talking! Oh, god, here I was in a hit show that was going to run forever. People had read reviews about the fabulous monologue, and I couldn't do it any more! I didn't know what to do. I was appalled. I tried harder and harder to recapture the feeling to no avail. I was in a state. When I knew the monologue was coming, I'd try to think of everything I could to get myself going emotionally. Nothing worked. The truth was *I* was now bored by the monologue. I'd said it over and over again in rehearsal and during the three weeks before we opened. Now, six weeks later, having done it about two hundred times, I just didn't care any more. So what? Been there, done that. But I was in a hit show. What to do?

After some days of torturing myself, I got the flu. Because my understudy wasn't ready, I had to go on stage with a temperature of around 104 degrees. I was almost delirious. By the end of the play, I didn't care that I couldn't do the monologue or whether the audience was bored or not. Screw it. I just wanted to get it over with and go home to bed. I sank into the chair, saying the words, but really communicating through them all the fever and sweating and sickness I felt. I wasn't trying to do it well or right. I was just being where I was. I was so ill that the experience was surreal. To my great surprise, I noticed that the audience seemed moved! They were really paying attention to me. I could see the tears coursing down rapt faces once more. Pocketbooks snapped open. I was stunned, frankly. I couldn't stop thinking about it when I went home. "Wow," I thought. "I wasn't feeling at *all* what I thought I should be feeling, yet the monologue moved the audience. How strange!"

I was still ill the next night, but I decided to try something. "What if I let myself be exactly where I am and just put it into the words?" It was a private little experiment. To my surprise, the monologue worked again. I took on this experiment like a scientist. "I'm going to see what happens if I just let myself feel whatever I feel—and not try to feel what I think I *should* feel." One night I was feeling extremely happy for whatever reason. I was certain that wasn't going to suit the monologue, but I let my happiness speak through the words. Lo and behold! Pocketbooks snapped. Tears coursed. No one read programs. It was a deliciously designed experiment, given that the audience thought they were invisible and therefore felt no compunction to be nice and pretend I was interesting. A fellow actor would have continued to pretend interest, but the audience did not lie. They didn't have to. They were dead honest in their reactions.

I expanded my experiment. Early in the show I played a character called Mrs. Saunders. The hilarious Jeffrey Jones and I made one entrance from behind the audience. I remember standing there trying to prepare, thinking about the scene that was about to happen on stage. I had the sudden thought, "Oh, why don't you just let yourself be here *now*, and trust that you'll be there *then*. Why are you trying to be *there* now? Just be here *now* and be there *then*."

Simple and maybe obvious as the idea was, it was novel to me. I remember relaxing completely and smiling to myself as I looked at the backs of the heads of the audience and heard them laughing about something that was happening on stage. I loved that moment. Everything became very sharp: the feel of my costume, the smell of the theater, my vision. Our cue came and off we went. The scene was fine. "Hey," I thought, "if it is okay to feel whatever I feel, I can do this play for a long time!" And I did. I relaxed and enjoyed the run. For more than a year I let myself feel whatever I felt as I acted. This was not what I had been taught by acting teachers, but it was wondrous to me how well it worked. If I slipped and tried to do the monologue *well* or feel what I wasn't feeling, it didn't work. What a relief that was to me as an actress!

While it was in *Cloud 9* that I learned the importance of Being Present and what it actually meant, it was through teaching that I learned about Being Present in greater depth. To emphasize the importance of Being Present, let's take a look at its opposite.

NOT BEING PRESENT

It is uncomfortable being around people who are not present. You can't wait to get away from them. They seem to suck all the air out of the space. They're not really *here*. Their minds flit around. They talk about themselves incessantly. Sometimes they brag or they talk about their problems without really wanting to solve them. You don't feel seen by them or listened to. They aren't really interested in you. After being with them even on the phone, you feel drained. You want a nap. They are exhausting. They stick a psychic straw in your energy field and sip on your power. I call them Energy Vampires. They are not present.

People who cannot be in their bodies act out in one of two ways:

> *1. Denial.* They go unconscious, go to sleep, go "south," eat, drink, go for any addiction, become defensive, suppress, and pretend that nothing is wrong. "I'm fine. I'm not angry. I don't care." They end up going out of communication with others and becoming isolated. They feel depressed and dead.
>
> *2. Dumping.* They make someone else responsible for what they feel. They blame other people. "You're making me angry. You're the problem. If you didn't _____, I wouldn't _____. You're so dominating." They may even scream in rage or beat their children. They dump their emotions irresponsibly and terrifyingly all over the people around them. These people end up at war in their relationships, in their jobs, and with the world. They are highly reactive and negative. They project their feelings onto others.

At the far end of the spectrum, an inability to feel can result in insanity and criminality. Not having a clue how to be with and own feelings means people end up acting them out in destructive ways.

Certainly you don't want to become insane, or a criminal, or an Energy Vampire. Because Energy Vampires don't know they are Energy Vampires, how do you know if *you* have a tendency to be one? Ask yourself how much you are afflicted with negative judgment, addiction, conflict, dishonesty, distraction, comparison, doubt, expectation, procrastination, perfectionism, worry, confusion, denial, righteousness, cynicism, and obsession. Reread the list carefully, and make an honest assessment.

We all have or do all these things to a degree, but the more we are troubled with them, the less we are present.

Maybe you are not as present as you thought you were.

If you aren't present, other people are paying the price for you. Feelings do not go away. They are in the air and the energy surrounding you. So if you don't feel your feelings, everyone else around you will.

You may have already made an effort to be present. Maybe you've had therapy, traveled to India, done many workshops, and still find it difficult. Don't judge yourself or your efforts, because it is *very difficult* to be present.

As a human being you have been as thoroughly trained *not* to be present as you were trained not to poop in public. You learned that exhibiting your feelings is a social taboo and that the less you do that, the more socially acceptable you are. Winners, champions, royalty do not show their feelings ever, if possible. "Never let them see you sweat." Poor losers and people who show disappointment are judged. You learned to smile when you didn't feel like it. I have witnessed many, many students feeling angry or fearful or sad only to belie these otherwise obvious feelings by smiling.

Culturally you have been taught to admire people who do not express their emotions, to admire stoics and people who can grin and bear it. By the time we are adults, most of us have such blunted feelings we sometimes don't even know *what* we are feeling.

On the other hand, if we had not been so well-trained, we would be like the kid in a funny Belgian television advertisement who throws a major tantrum in a store tearing groceries off their shelves, hurling himself to the floor, kicking and screaming because he's not getting his "sweeties." His father is crushed with embarrassment. Other customers are horrified. At the end of the commercial appears the slogan, "Use condoms."

Without our training, we would all be like that little kid, except fully grown, grabbing what we want and killing whoever got in the way—which some people do.

It is a conundrum because we have to be trained and civilized in order to live together in as much peace as we manage. The problem is we learn not just to control our emotions but to stifle them and think of them as bad. Some of us, myself included, become deeply depressed (suppressed) as a result. Or, we use whatever artificial means (drugs, sex, video games) to control, deny, and remove ourselves from feeling. We are trained to think not to feel. Unfortunately, our thinking gets completely fouled up by unfelt feelings. Unless we are lucky to have had parents who understand how to help us feel our feelings without suppressing them or acting them out, we will end up doing one or the other having no real understanding of how to *have* our feelings fully without acting out.

So we learn to suppress our feelings. But the truth is that our feelings do not just go away. When feelings are suppressed, they eventually turn inward to self-hatred or outward in attack. We seem to know only those two choices. Feelings will come out one way or another—as disease or war. Therefore, it is vital to our very survival to redo our training by learning how to have our feelings rather than suppress them or attack others.

Additionally, ask yourself if you are following your true path. Take a moment to honestly assess if there is something you want to be doing that you are not doing. Or are you doing many things that you really don't want to do, living a life that you don't want to live? If so, don't berate yourself; don't use it as another opportunity to criticize yourself, expect perfection, or blame others. Instead, devote yourself to becoming more present—one moment at a time—so that you may be guided to your heart's desires. Being Present is the key to discovering what your heart really wants and needs. Being Present is the key to being truly alive.

How does one do that?

THE QUESTION

I discovered one simple question that I ask students in classes and in my workshops. It is an unfailing key to becoming present: *What sensation are you experiencing in your body right now?* I don't know when I first asked it, but I have asked the question to actors and participants in my workshops thousands of times. I still find the results awesome, delightful, healing, mysterious, and endlessly fascinating.

It is such a simple question but who ever asks you that question? Yes, they may ask, "What are you feeling?" And you may respond, "Scared," "Tired," "Depressed," "Happy," "Sad," and so on. *Where do you feel scared in your body?* elicits quite a different response that is much more specific.

What sensation are you experiencing in your body right now? is a powerful and difficult question because it requires one to feel uncomfortable sensations. It is not a popular question. I doubt it ever will be. People resist it—even the people I teach in class. When students acknowledge what they are feeling in their bodies, they are allowing themselves to feel exposed and seen by others in all their fear and vulnerability. There is no way to maintain a cover or pretend to be cool when talking about a jelly feeling in the belly. It takes a lot of courage to talk about shaky legs, a raw feeling in the chest, or feeling fat around the thighs.

Actors must be as authentic and real as they can to get jobs. They *know* they have to open up if they want to be good actors, so as a teacher, I have a built-in permission to ask this difficult question.

The question is vital because it allows you to Be Present with the barriers that are in the way of your movement along your path. We get stuck in life. The way to get unstuck is to feel the places where we are stuck. The results are quite miraculous. The barriers dissolve, melt, disappear, and we are free to move forward again.

What sensation are you experiencing in your body right now? I advise you not to jump at your friends with this question. They may not like it. It is the ultimate of *intimacy. Into-me-see.* Get it? Even with my best friends who know the question, I approach gently when they are upset. "Would you like to Get Present around it?" I ask. If the answer is no, I don't press it. Only in class do I have *carte blanche* to ask the question.

THE BODY

The body is a better source of truth than the brain. It is said that we use only a small percentage of our brains. Perhaps it is because we are missing our greatest source of information and creativity: the body. One of the brain's jobs is to guard the survival and maintenance of the body, so it will lie to you, and often does, in order to maintain the *status quo* and keep you "safe."

Most of us have been trained to be in our minds. We spend much of our time trying to control life, dominate it, figure it out, look good, and win. We're terrified of our bodies. In truth, any decision that is made without consulting our bodies is a dangerous one: our minds are too well-trained in denial and deceit.

The body is the real channel of information and creativity. Its language is sensation. Everything we need to know is stored in or channeled through the body. Goethe said that nothing can be truly learned unless it is experienced. It is the body that experiences—not the brain—which, interestingly enough, has no sensation at all: the brain itself feels nothing, poor thing. Maybe the brain is jealous of the body, and this competition is the problem.

In an article about incest and memory in *The Northeast Recovery Networker*, Dr. Jeanne C. Folks states, "If the mind were just a sophisticated recording device, then memory would have little to do with feelings. But the mind does not work alone in the process of recording life experiences. The mind is only a servant of the larger ruling order of memory within the psyche—the body. Memories can exist in the body, apart from the conscious mind."

In her book *Breaking Down the Wall of Silence*, Alice Miller writes, "Anyone who has experienced how the truth stored in our bodies can be located and evaluated with remarkable precision, will...no longer be prepared to put up the evasions and excuses."

Sensation is information and should be validated and welcomed—including pain. *Lest someone misinterpret my statement, let me hasten to add that pain does not need to be sought or inflicted on oneself or others. I'm talking about sensations that come up naturally, on their own.*

"UNACCEPTABLE" FEELINGS

In my teaching and my workshops, I have discovered that there is a sensation or set of sensations that most of us would do anything to avoid rather than experience, and *we construct our entire lives around trying to not have those particular sensations.*

For example, one of my students could not bear the sensation of feeling trapped. So instead of going deeply into feeling trapped, what she has done all her life is pack up her things and move to another place. But as soon as she gets to another place, she thinks some other place will be better, so she moves again to avoid feeling trapped. Of course the new place is never good enough, and she still struggles with feeling trapped. The problem is that she also longs for security and a home, but she hasn't been able to stay in one place long enough to create one for herself. Eventually, she chose to go deeply into the sensation of feeling trapped when it came up. As a result, she is now able to make wiser decisions, and she is now able to settle down.

Michael is a very talented actor who hated feeling "comfortable." It made him think he was "big, dumb, and stupid." Somewhere along the line he believed that he couldn't possibly be talented if he weren't suffering. Because he couldn't accept the feeling of being calm and at ease in his body, he constructed his life to be one of constant drama and crisis. He did not really like all that drama, but hadn't been able to change it. After accepting feeling comfortable, the drama in his life calmed down considerably.

WEATHERING SENSATIONS

There are palettes full of sensations that people resist. Exhaustion was mine. The exhaustion always felt physical. I never believed it was emotional. However, when I went deeply into the exhaustion and really felt it and expressed it, I discovered an intense grief and a feeling of defeat underneath that went back to my infancy. I am now better able to withstand discouragement without becoming completely defeated and stopped.

Exhaustion covers many feelings. Often in class, actors feel exhausted *before* working. If they don't resist it, when they begin the scene or monologue, feelings come bursting out. Then, after they're finished acting, they feel quite energized and the exhaustion is gone.

Oddly enough, the sensation that seems utterly unbearable to me may be okay with you. Among such sensations are: cold, heat, numbness, calm, tiredness, tingling, stillness, deadness, ease, pressure, tension, being turned on, being turned off, excitement, joy, relaxation, constriction, nausea, stillness, stuckness, dizziness, floating, emptiness, etc.

In all cases, sensations are merely sensations and are transformed from terrifying to benign once they are experienced.

The transformation is much like opening a closet only to discover that the monster scratching against the door is just a branch brushing up against the house.

There isn't a person I've worked with who doesn't fear that he will die if he opens the door and experiences the terrifying sensation. But none has. In fact, the thought "I'm dying" or "I'll die if I experience this" may be a clear signal that you're at the right door.

Sensations may seem generalized at first, but as awareness increases, they become localized in vulnerable parts of the body: the skin, the hands, the feet, the groin, the mouth, the eyes, the cheeks, the head, the neck, the back, the legs, the feet, the stomach, and frequently, the heart or the trunk of the body.

Unfortunately, the sensations we particularly hate will probably come up more often for us than for anyone else. Everything in our lives seems to conspire to get us to feel what we don't want to feel.

Resistance creates persistence. When we resist, we are not free. We struggle to get away from, fix, or change what we feel. Like Chinese finger cuffs that tighten when you try to pull your fingers apart, the cuffs come off when you do the opposite—put the fingers together. It is the same with feeling: *the only way out is in—into the body.*

The reason the sensations that we particularly hate pop up so frequently is that we never go into them all the way. We resist them with all our might. "I don't want to feel this!" "I feel this all the time!" "This is a very old feeling!" "I hate this!" "I want to get through this!" "I want to get beyond this!" "This is stupid!" "This is silly!" But this is just standing at the door. The most we do is rattle the doorknob and yell at the sensation to go away. People often forget that the point of Being Present is not to get *rid* of what they are feeling. That is setting the process askew. The point of Being Present is to be *present.* Don't struggle at the door. Open it and go in.

FEAR

Alaska Natives have many words for different types of snow. I would like two words to distinguish between sensation-fear and thought-fear. Although they are connected, they can be separated. In fact, one way to master fear is to feel the sensations but not feed them with fearful thoughts.

We react to fear in several ways: stuffing it down, turning it into anger, or feeding it with fearful thoughts ending up in panic. Denying fear is dangerous. If there is a devil, he likes to hide in difficult-to-see places—like viruses, odorless poisons, and unexperienced fear.

Fear is not the devil. Not being willing to be with fear is the problem. Fear that is experienced but not acted upon harms no one. The people who do the most damage in the world are not even aware that they are afraid. They will attack physically or verbally rather than feel their own fear. They will make *you* feel their fear rather than feel it themselves. The results are attack and domination. Attackers may not feel remorse. They may feel quite justified and satisfied because they have saved themselves from the terrifying *experience* of fear once again.

As an alerting devise to keep us safe from wild animals, fires, and crawling out onto tiny branches in tall trees, fear is effective. But fear pops up when our survival is not threatened. We live in fear overdrive. Our minds find every intense feeling to be threatening—anything that is not the *status quo*. We are just as afraid of good things happening—great success, happiness, ecstasy because these things make our bodies feel extraordinary sensations. Our minds want us to live within a small corridor of "safe" sensations.

What is more fearless than a tiny kitten or a baby? We learn to be afraid. By our teen-age years, our highly developed fears can virtually shut us down. We may become so sophisticated in our ability to avoid anything fearful that we can end up shut down and shut away in safe, little, mental, emotional, and physical cubicles. If fear does increase with age, that is all the more reason to become friends with it.

If you look at thought-fear, you see that it is really about the future. F.E.A.R. Future Events Appear Ruinous. We make it all up in our minds. We sit in our cozy living rooms and drive ourselves crazy with fear. We dive into thoughts about aloneness, death, illness, poverty, and dig our own hole to hell. It all looks absolutely real—even though the future truly is the unknown and unknowable—even the next minute.

It is what we don't know that can scare us. Makers of horror films know that the audience will be more frightened of what they don't see on screen than what they actually do see. Amusingly, in the movies the point-of-view of the hand-held camera is *us*. *We* are the unknown, terrible monster creeping down the hall.

Once we make up fear in our minds, our bodies are thrown into turmoil. Our bodies, being so dense (as in solid rather than stupid), hold onto and store emotions. As a child, when I was afraid, my mother would say dismissively, "Oh, stop being afraid. There is nothing to be afraid of." Although that may have been perfectly true, it was too late. I was already feeling intense fear. Telling yourself not to be afraid when you *are* afraid is not going to help. Feeling fear without listening to negative thoughts, without making decisions, or without drawing conclusions will move you through the fear.

We make it more difficult for ourselves by inventing so much of our fear and then trying to avoid or suppress feeling it. "I'm not afraid. I just don't feel like going to that audition, calling that agent, getting up in front of the class, going into my own business, or loving you."

That's the bad news. The good news is that fear can be mastered. But the path to mastery is different than we think it is. We think if we wait long enough, fear will go away, or we can talk ourselves out of it, or find ways to conquer it. During World War II, Franklin Delano Roosevelt famously declared, "We have nothing to fear but fear itself." Ultimately, it is not fear that stops us. It is being afraid of fear that stops us. We are so afraid of fear that we will do anything to avoid that experience. *When we are willing to experience fear without attaching it to people, ideas, and things, we have mastered fear.*

What is it that we are afraid of? In working with myself, my students, and participants in my workshop, it is apparent that fear of fear is really fear of physical sensation. Most of us detest the physical sensations provoked by what we call intense fear. When thought-fear causes us to feel sensation-fear, we will do everything we can to physically remove ourselves from the sensations. I have seen people in my workshops literally try to get out of their own bodies—hopping backward, wriggling, crouching, twisting, turning—doing anything to escape from experiencing the physical sensations of fear.

As John Patrick Shanley said, "Everything worthwhile in life requires just a little bit more courage than we currently have." This means if we are to keep moving forward on our path, we must make friends with fear. Fear of the unknown, of the next breakthrough, of the next big challenge will never go away.

What happens when one is willing to experience the physical sensations of fear? It can be quite miraculous. People become literally transformed right in front of your eyes. What was impossible a moment before becomes not only possible, but natural. A student once said beautifully, "Fear, instead of being the baby sitter I always thought it was, is really like wild geese calling me home through landscapes I never would have traveled on my own."

ANGER/RAGE

Anger feels better than fear to some people. So some people may slip into anger or rage rather than feel their fear. I see it happen often with men, because in most cultures the world over, men are taught they are not supposed to feel fear. But it is men who can't allow themselves to feel terror who beat their wives, gnash their teeth, and start wars. It is tragic that men are not trained to own their fear. I am grateful to every man who has allowed his fear to be seen in my workshops and classes. They give me hope for the world.

Of course, it is not just men who are unwilling to feel their fear and let it be seen. One time I was at a party with Anna, a dear friend. Every once in a while she would go to the phone and call her teen-age daughter to check up on her, but her daughter didn't answer the phone. Anna became more and more frightened. Just before she decided to leave the party and go home, she called one more time. The daughter answered. Immediately, Anna bawled her out. I was wide-eyed as I listened to her rage build, and I could hear her daughter scream back at her mother over the phone. I put my hand on Anna's arm. "Just tell her how scared you were," I whispered softly, hoping she would not bite my head off, too. Anna's eyes welled up and she burst into tears. She took a breath and told her daughter how she felt. They stopped fighting.

Anger can be either a step toward health or away from health depending on the individual. If one uses it as a justification for attack, either outwardly or inwardly, obviously anger is not a healthy response. If one can use anger as energy to act in a healthy but non-attacking way, then it is useful.

Many actors are afraid to feel intense anger and rage, but often, when they can just *have* anger without doing anything destructive, it will be transformed into its essence: power to act, to choose, to create, to be passionate about one's life, to take charge, to take a stand. All the energy for life is inherent in our anger and rage if we can stand in the power of it non-destructively. Rage is like nuclear energy. You can use it to blow up a city or light it up. It is your choice whether to destroy your life or empower it.

GRIEF

Grief is an expression of our love. It is a way of letting go. Some people will not allow themselves to grieve. Their dog or cat gets sick and dies, and they can't allow themselves be sad or grief-stricken. They rant and rave that life sucks and there is no God—because it is too difficult to experience the grief. We feel deeply about things. We're supposed to feel deeply if we're alive and participating in life—being vulnerable, opening our hearts, loving, losing. That's the way it is.

I fell in love with the Dalai Lama based on something he said in an interview when he was asked how he dealt with the death of his beloved brother. He answered very simply, "I was very sad for a long time, and then, gradually I was not so sad." He didn't berate himself for being too attached to his brother. He didn't try not to feel.

DESPAIR/DEPRESSION

Unfortunately, our culture has a very low tolerance for despair and depression. We sweep depression under the carpet, neaten up the room, and paste on smiley-face masks. We approach depressed people as if there is something very wrong with them. "Don't give in to despair! Wrestle it to the ground! Get up and *do* something! What's *wrong* with you? Take some pills! Take more pills!" We are scared to death of depression and despair. We prefer violence to despair. At least violent people can kick ass. Depressed people are losers. We afflict ourselves with commercials, and movies, and self-help books that try to obliterate one of the most potent tools of the psyche.

I read somewhere that depression is actually gestation. Depression as gestation is a very powerful context. I believe it is true. Abraham Lincoln, Winston Churchill, and Anwar Sadat were often depressed. Perhaps their depressions correlated to their powers. The dark nights of the soul can be powerful journeys. I call such journeys "trips to the dark side of the moon." Sometimes we fall out of communication with ourselves, others, and even God. But if we can make the trip consciously, there is always a treasure to be found. And when we circle back into the light, there is an enormous power surge. We become stronger than before.

But it is difficult: a vacation in hell. "I don't want anything," despair says. "I see no point in anything! It is all sound and fury signifying nothing!" It is all NO. Despair is a fact of life. We all have our dark nights of the soul. It is what we do with them that counts. Despair is one of the reasons I am so grateful to God for making humans creators and artists: *we can turn despair into art*. We are true alchemists. We take life's lead and turn it into gold. Where else does that happen?

William Shakespeare's *Timon of Athens* is about a man in a train-wreck of despair and depression. Fortunately, our literature continues to teach us to have compassion toward those in despair. Sometimes we can even take despair and pain and turn it into comedy. Clowns paint tears on their faces and then do pratfalls. Christopher Durang, Anton Chekhov, and Neil Simon, to mention a few playwrights, use pain and despair as grist for their comedic mills.

When we can be brave enough not to resist certain kinds of depression, we may not have to stay with it as long. A young woman in class had been in a struggle about her career for a long time. One day she could no longer resist her despair, but she was terrified of feeling her feelings, because she believed that she would actually go crazy and never come back. I encouraged her by saying that she only had to touch her despair—in her mind's eye to reach out and touch it to get a sense of the size and depth of it. She did.

Her experience was not very dramatic on the outside. She did not gnash her teeth and writhe on the floor. She was slumped over and quiet, but it was clear that she was in it and not resisting it. After about half a minute, she lifted her head. "Did you touch it?" I asked.

"Yeah," she answered and that was that. The class continued. After class, she and I happened to walk down the street together. She was laughing and chatting. She was surprised that she felt so light. Indeed, she called me several days later and said that her despair was just "gone," and she felt she could follow her career once more.

I was depressed for many years, but had no one to help me be with it consciously—to allow it and to validate it. Phrases like "Snap out of it! What's wrong with you?!" were all I heard. I used all my energy fighting to control my depression. Of course, it didn't work. I was nearly always tired and exhausted from the internal battle.

About ten years ago, I woke up in that black, horrible, familiar state. I felt beaten up. I staggered into my living room where a friend was having her morning coffee. I slumped into a chair. The weight of my depression pressed me down into it. I could feel my automatic response to want to get rid of it, fight it, and chastise myself for it. With my friend's help, I stopped resisting my depression and got present with it. I gave into it completely and consciously experienced it in my body.

My depression felt heavy—as if there were a lead blanket covering my whole body. I could see it vividly. It was black rubber—flat black. It was precisely 3/16 of an inch thick. The surface of it was a shiny, much- wrinkled, metallic green as if it had been used for a long time. It seemed to weigh 150 pounds. I couldn't move under it. What an old, familiar childhood feeling—dead and pressed down.

As I identified the characteristics of the lead blanket, I began to see the purpose it had served in my childhood: it had protected me from invisible but deadly rays—from things I could not see, feel, hear, smell, or know through any of my senses. It had done its job. It was sturdy and reliable. It was impenetrable and practically indestructible. I could trust it. I could surrender to it. The lethal radiation had not killed me. I had survived my childhood. My depression had actually protected me!

But I no longer needed it. It was much too heavy to carry around. What had saved me in childhood was now debilitating me. I thanked it profoundly and blessed it and myself for inventing such an effective survival technique. I felt it lift off me. I cried with relief. I have never felt that kind of depression since that day. The whole process took only about twenty minutes.

Loving yourself when you are in despair, weak, lost, or feeling like a failure is the deepest self-love. Let's face it: we love characters in literature when they plunge to the depths or are less than superhuman. Such characters are the roles that always win Oscars. Wouldn't it be wonderful if we could be as compassionate with ourselves as we are with Willy Loman in *Death of a Salesman* or Blanche DuBois in *A Streetcar Named Desire*?

ILLNESS

Even illness often has within it a great gift if we can open ourselves to it and let go of resistance. We tend to think of illness as something that has gone wrong. We blame ourselves and lament, "What did I do to create this?!" Although we do need to take whatever steps necessary to get well and healthy, a more empowering question is, "What is this illness doing for me that I haven't been able to do for myself?"

God knows how much my flu contributed to me in my *Cloud 9* experience. Every time I've been sick and had to perform on stage it has helped me enormously to relax and let go of control. Sickness can loosen our grip. Many of my greatest lessons in acting have come when I have been too ill to maintain my tension. I had to relax in order to just get through a performance.

Sometimes it is not easy to do in the midst of illness. Maybe one can see the benefit of an illness only in retrospect—unless you are a master of life like Ram Dass, who called his debilitating stroke "Fierce Grace."

Bill, a student of mine, was a national downhill-skiing champion. He was scheduled to be in a very big race. It terrified him. All his heroes were going to be in it. He had competed in the race many times without winning or even coming close to winning. Something always stopped him. When he got to the hotel before the event, he became ill, and was up all night with a fever of 104. He was too sick to scout the course beforehand. Bill almost pulled out of the race, but decided to do it anyway.

Although the outside temperature was a warm fifty degrees, he had to bundle up in heavy, bulky clothing. He completely gave up the idea of winning, but got in line anyway. One of his heroes scored a great time. Bill felt no pressure because there was no hope. When it was his turn, he raced down the hill. On the trip down, he heard a train whistle. He was mesmerized by it and felt himself pulled by the whistle down the hill. He had no thought about winning. He wasn't *trying*.

Of course, he won. He was amazed and astonished, but he won! His illness had guided him to let go completely.

"What is this illness doing for me that I haven't done for myself?" may be a difficult question initially, but it is a fruitful one when you can ask it with calm and interest. Ram Dass said that his stroke taught him how to accept support—something he had found very difficult to do in the past.

LOVE

Some of the most difficult sensations to be with are those associated with love—of feeling the heart widely and wildly open. Terrifying. Just to stand in the presence of the feelings of love takes enormous courage—courage to have the feelings and share them without grabbing onto someone or something or projecting onto someone or something.

A young man once burst into an office where I was sitting. He was radiating an infectious joy.

"Man," he said, "I am so in love! Wow! I'm wildly in love!"

"Great!" I said.

"Yeah," he responded smiling broadly. "All I need is someone to give it to!"

I laughed but I got it. I was impressed. He knew that his feelings of love were his. Someone may definitely trigger love feelings, but truthfully, they are no more the *cause* of our feelings of love than our feelings of rage, sadness, or any other feeling. When we feel the moments of great love in our lives, there is usually someone there to be the recipient and caretaker/guardian of the feelings. But the more intense the feelings, the more terrifying it is when the person goes away. We are left to feel the sensations all by ourselves. When we can't accept the intense feelings of vulnerability, excitement, and aliveness, love can turn into obsession and possessiveness. It can become about ownership. It can turn into addiction.

BREAKTHROUGH

When we are willing to feel, the result will be Breakthrough. The mind does not like a breakthrough or real change. It likes the *status quo*. It wants us to be safe, secure, and quiet. The mind resists change. Judgment becomes particularly strong when the mind is threatened with change.

In contrast, once one understands the process of Breakthrough and Change, one can learn to ride them more gracefully like a surfer on a wave. Breakthrough goes a bit like birth:

1. Discomfort that gets worse and worse until there is:

2. Birth or Breakthrough that is usually sudden and causes:

3. Freakout, because we are in territory that we have never experienced before, so we:

4. Backup—or try to backup until we:

5. Get familiar with the new territory, until discomfort begins to build toward a new Breakthrough.

In the process of Breakthrough, there is a period of gestation. The closer one gets to Breakthrough, the greater the discomfort. The bigger the Breakthrough, the more unfamiliar is the new territory.

New babies frequently lose weight just after birth, perhaps because they are totally freaked out. "Oh, my God. Where am I? I'm used to warm, wet, dark walls, the thump of that heart, and eating through my stomach. Here things are bright and dry. There are no walls—just lots of strange noises, and I have to eat through my mouth! The problem was I got too big. I don't care HOW uncomfortable that old place was. I'm going to stop eating and go back! Waaaaaaaaah!"

A quantum leap is a kind of Breakthrough. If enough heat (discomfort) is applied to an electron in an atom, it makes a sudden leap to another orbit, hangs out there getting acquainted with the new territory, until it may be heated some more and make another jump.

As a teacher, what I find interesting about the dynamics of Breakthrough is that the place I am most likely to lose a student, meaning a student stops coming to class, is in the period of Freakout. That's when a student may go away. If a student has just had a tremendous breakthrough in acting, suddenly he may disappear. And he will justify it in all kinds of seemingly logical, rational ways. I've had students get sick, have physical injuries—all kinds of things happen—and no matter how much I warn them about the process, it still happens.

LEVELS OF BEING PRESENT IN THE BODY

Being with the sensations of the body both unleashes emotional suppression and stops emotional addiction. Whichever happens—emotional expression or a calming down of emotionality—the result will be truly authentic.

When getting present, people who are blocked emotionally will express feelings openly. Then there are people who have been labeled hypersensitive and overly dramatic. They are emotional addicts—an addict being someone who can never get enough. Oddly, although others may think of such people as feeling too much, in truth they haven't been present at all—they haven't felt enough. They have such a hard time simply being in the sensations of their bodies that one has to walk on egg shells through the mine fields of their unfelt feelings. God forbid you should step on one of their delicate emotional hair-triggers and set off an explosion. Don't shake them up. They're emotional nitroglycerine. They are sitting on so much rage that when they explode volcanically, you had better run before you get caught in their lava stream.

However, when hypersensitive people learn to be truly present, the results are astonishing. They become calmer and more willing to go deep into the feelings in their bodies. They become coherent, where before they became present, one could barely understand what they were saying. And it is not that they are feeling less; it is actually that they are feeling more.

The Mind Is Unconnected to the Body

In response to the question *What sensation are you experiencing in your body right now?* people who are unconnected and unacquainted with their bodies, will respond directly from their minds, thinking that they are talking about sensation. Their responses are thought-oriented, even though they may use the word *feel.* "I feel stupid." "I feel like I'm taking up too much time." "I feel silly." "I feel like I'm going to fail." Such declarations are *not* feelings. They are thoughts—judgments from the mind about unexperienced sensation. The mind. *Yattatta yattatta.* Getting people out of their minds and into their bodies is like trying to pull gum off cotton balls: consciousness has been so trained to stick so close to thought instead of feeling.

It is necessary to retrain one's use of language and not use the word *feel* when the accurate word is *think*. "I think I am stupid." "I think I am taking up too much time." "I think I'm silly." "I think I'm going to fail."

This disconnectedness is often a response to fear and panic that manifests in obsessive thinking. Betty, a friend of mine, used to be one of the most disconnected people I've ever known. When she was upset, she would rattle on and on, never actually experiencing what she felt. I found it hilarious at times, and I wrote a character in a play based on her characteristic of not actually being present. Sometimes, though, it was not amusing because her inability to be present intensified and lengthened her suffering.

One time, after cancer surgery, she talked for days—raging obsessively about the behavior of her boyfriend. Never once did she acknowledge her terror about cancer. It was very hard to listen to her obsessive thoughts. At that time, before I understood the particular mechanism, I tried to help her deal with the issue of her boyfriend. It was a totally hopeless and pointless endeavor—like digging a tunnel with a teaspoon. I was so caught in the drama about her boyfriend that I wasn't aware that her obsession was an indication of her unexperienced fear.

Many years later after I had learned much more about Being Present with the sensations of the body, she took my workshop. At one point, she burst out, "Now I know what you've been talking about! It is simple! It is easy!"

Some months later, we were traveling in a blizzard. I was following her car in mine. Her car slipped off the road and stopped. There was no collision, but by the time I pulled off the road and walked back to her car, she was in a panic.

Again she started rattling maniacally, making judgments about life, BMW's, herself, snow, and Connecticut. Because she was in a genuine panic, I resisted my impulse to laugh at her unintentionally comic monologue. Instead, I asked her what she was experiencing in her body. She hated the question but grudgingly told me about what she was feeling in her body. Within minutes she was calm, and we were able to proceed. She had gone through the fear.

A good rule of thumb to remember is simply: *We are never upset about what we think we're upset about.* The more upset we are, the deeper the real issue. When we can allow the sensations that will lead us to the real issue, we will become calmer.

Connected at the Level of Emotion

At the next level, students say, "I'm scared." "I feel angry." "I feel sad." Although the emotional identification is a marked advance from mind chatter, it is general and is not Being Present in the specific body sensations. But it is a beginning.

When people say they feel scared, I ask them where in their bodies they experience that fear. At first, most people are astonished at the question. No one ever asked them to be that anatomically specific before—to look at feeling scared that closely. Initially, they'll say, "All over. I feel scared all over."

When I ask them where they feel scared the most, they begin to get conscious. It is fascinating to watch someone examine the sensations in his or her body for the first time. There is a wide range of experience for all the generalized emotions such as fear, anger, and love. "My hands are cold." "My hands are hot and sweaty." "My shoulder muscles feel rigid." "My knees are locked." "Pain in the center of my back (my stomach, my forehead, etc.)" "My legs are shaking." And on and on.

Body and Mind Connected

The body is immensely creative and elegant in its intelligence. That is not to say that Being Present is anti-brain or anti-thinking. Far from it. When the body and brain are aligned, genius emerges. When the brain tries to dominate and disregard the body, there is suffering. Imagery is the marriage of mind and body. It is the mind's creative interpretation of bodily sensation. It is the ultimate in creativity and healing. In response to the question "What sensations are you experiencing right now?" some students will respond in images. "There's a very sharp pain right in the center of my diaphragm. Right there—like a tube. It is red and black—sometimes red, sometimes black—and hollow. Very hard—like steel." Such imagery frequently happens when sensation is consciously experienced.

"There's a sensation in my forehead of weight. Like something is pulling it down. Like there's this heavy rock hanging down. It is pulling my whole being down with it."

"Let yourself really experience it," I say, never knowing if it is going to intensify or lessen.

When consciously experiencing sensation, the sensations that are in the way will decrease, and those that have information will increase.

When the mind and body are working together, often there are "unpleasant" images that emerge from the sensations: "a foot stepping on my heart," "drowning," "a little man running around in my stomach," "thousands of hands pressing out." As a person reaches out and accepts these images, the images transform. The "foot" becomes "the foot of God trying to open up my heart." "Drowning" becomes pleasant, "like being immersed in warm, clear water." The "little man" becomes a cute elf creating fun things. The "hands" become "helping hands."

The more I work with people in classes and workshops, the more astonished I am at the elegance and intelligence of the body/mind when it is aligned. I could cite thousands of examples of the healing that occurs when this happens.

To demonstrate how organic this process is, the following happened with a woman whom I barely knew who had no prior knowledge of this work at all and was on four different kinds of medicine prescribed by a battery of psychiatrists and therapists. She was anorexic, hypersensitive, and had been addicted to almost everything.

One morning after a meeting we attended together, she told me she was in a panic. She felt herself slipping into a dark hole. She was crying, nearly hysterical. I found myself alone with her. The others had left. Without any prompting from me, she said, "It is in my bowels—this dark, awful hole, and all these demons are in my bowels." She was verging toward real panic. So I did what I do: I asked her if she would be willing to experience what was going on in her bowels and to describe it to me.

At first, when she went to the center of the feeling, she was terrified. "My guts are getting bigger and bigger! They're going to explode!" she cried out. Being emotionally addicted, she stared panicking even more.

"See if you can stay with the feelings in your guts and let them explode," I persisted. She did as I suggested and immediately calmed down. She took a deep breath, relaxed and stayed with the image. "What's happening now?" I asked.

"It is—ooo—it is like I'm nine months pregnant." Already her willingness to experience and accept the sensation had created a more benign image, but she resisted again. "Oooo," she cried more. "I want to push it out!!!"

"See if you can just let yourself be nine months pregnant." Again she relaxed and her emotions subsided. She sat for a moment.

"In your mind's eye," I said, "touch your stomach. See if you can accept it."

After a moment, she smiled. "It is very taut. It is nice and pink." Again, she wanted to slip into negativity. "But there are all these voices and all this awful black gook. Oh, it is awful."

"Where is it?" I inquired.

"It is inside my stomach!" She squirmed.

"See if you can reach in and touch it," I suggested. She was very reluctant. "What does it feel like?" I asked.

"Slimy. Like jelly."

"Just feel it. Let yourself feel it."

"It doesn't have any color now." Again, the acceptance of it transformed it into a more benign image. "Oh!" she said suddenly. "There's a tiny little embryo in there. God, it is only a week old or—no. It is two weeks old." She was positive about its age.

"Can you touch it and hold it?" I ask.

"I can cradle it," she said.

"Can you accept it?" I asked.

"Yes," she said. She talked about the embryo and wanting to protect it. She was seeing it as herself—something that she wanted to and needed to take care of—this tiny, vulnerable, two-week-old embryo. The whole process didn't take long, maybe fifteen or twenty minutes, but she connected with her body in a way that she never had before, and it got her through that day at least.

Body and Mind Open to Wisdom

The phenomenon of finding within the sensations of the body all the information, healing, and wisdom one needs is not something that I have invented. It is something that I have observed. It happens spontaneously when one merely focuses and observes carefully what is being experienced in the body—just as it did with the woman and the embryo.

The body is Creation's message center. I mean this in both the literal and spiritual sense. God may not try to speak to us through our brains because most of us don't know how to listen. So, God (or The Big Whatever, as I call it) speaks through sensation.

What we need to know—all the information we need to have—is available in the sensations of our bodies. Our bodies are brilliant if we can learn how to be in them and listen to them. Once we are fully present, we become available to a wisdom far beyond our every day understandings.

During my workshops, accessing this wisdom began happening spontaneously, so I learned how to consciously include it in the process. Once we are Present, all we have to do is call upon our Higher Self or Higher Power to be with us. It doesn't matter whether you believe in God or not. This Wise Self, or Higher Power, or God is always available.

A woman in my workshop was stuck with the context that she could do nothing in life unless she was perfect. This idea kept her from pursuing almost anything.

My first response was to want to convince her to give up the notion that she had to be perfect, that her idea of perfection was too harsh—a pretty logical response. Fortunately, I kept my mouth shut and instead guided her to get present.

Immediately, she felt very fat. Unpleasant to her mind at first, eventually she let herself feel it completely. She sat cross-legged, wrists on her knees, and smiled broadly. She felt like Buddha—a smiling Buddha. She saw herself surrounded by hundreds of flowers and happy worshippers. She felt completely happy and at peace. Watching her, I was amazed. She seemed to glow as if there were a halo surrounding her.

Suddenly I saw the wisdom in what she was experiencing, and I nearly gasped. How wonderful. She didn't need to worry about being perfect. She *was* perfect! Buddha is the earthly personification of perfection. Her Buddha was letting her know her own perfection. What a wise and wonderful way to end her struggle with trying to be perfect.

Such wisdom is not intellectual. It is a knowledge found in the body and is accessible when we are fully present. Wisdom is inside *everyone*.

EXPERIENCING "NOTHING"

When people are asked what they feel in their bodies, sometimes they respond, "Nothing." There are three kinds of "Nothing" responses:

Dead Nothing

They say, "Nothin'." Unless one is dead, that is impossible. There are always physical sensations—the feel of the floor, clothing against the body, warmth, cold, tiny itches, etc. But some people are so trained to ignore their bodies that they simply cannot identify sensation unless it is exceptional pleasure or exceptional pain. That is depression—literally the depression of the sensations of the body.

The name for my two-day workshop, *The Creative Explosion,* came out of an experience with an actress. She was new to class. As she presented her Shakespearean monologue, my heart sank. She was giving a performance that was stock acting—completely phony, not spontaneous, and full of lifeless, premeditated gestures.

I asked myself, "How am I going to work with this?!" Fortunately, I have learned to be quiet when it comes to my judgments, and instead, I utilized the technique of Getting Present in working with her. I said, "Okay. Let's just do it again, but before we do, let's find out where you are physically."

At first she was unaware. "I feel nothing," she said. But as she focused, she became aware of sensation in her heart and stomach area—a tickling at first. Then it grew and kept growing until it became what she described as a red-hot fire burning in her very center.

I said, "Now you look present. Start communicating that speech from where you are—from fire in your heart and belly." She opened her mouth and was powerful, spontaneous, real, and deliciously dangerous. Her voice filled Shakespeare's words. She had become the queen. I was astonished at the totality of the transformation. It was as if she had exploded right in front of our eyes, and this had come from her body—not from any technique. She had at first delivered one of the worst performances I had ever seen, and then one of the best in very little time. We were all completely blown away. Thus, she created the possibility of

Breakthrough in acting that I had not seen before and given me the name for my workshop, *The Creative Explosion*.

Afterward, she could not stop crying. She was as stunned as the rest of us. She had never experienced acting in that way before. It had been exhilarating for her, but then terrifying. She kept repeating, "I don't know how that happened! How do I do that again?!" I gave her a hug, and told her to celebrate what had happened, rather than look for a way to control life again. I knew if she could do it once, she could do it again. And she has.

Non-significant Sensations

When I hear "Nothin'," I ask students to focus on their bodies like a scientist and to look around for any sensation, no matter how small or insignificant it may be. They describe a veritable symphony of sensations. "My hands are cold." "My lips are dry." "There's a weight on my shoulders between my shoulder blades." "There's a little pain in my left hip." "My cheeks feel like they're falling down." And on and on.

Some people are unsatisfied with that. They think they should feel more, something significant, something dramatic. Actors often cannot believe that they can act well from such a non-significant place. Yet, they can. One of the greatest learning experiences for an inexperienced actor is to watch brilliant actors just walk on stage and do it.

On the other hand, it is very uncomfortable to watch a young actor rev himself up, trying to dredge up emotion, mentally killing his loved ones in order to get the all-important tears going. The irony is that if actors would accept non-significant sensation, they would be fine.

So it is in life: We think we *have* to *feel* a certain way in order to do something. It is much simpler than that. *Know where you are and take a step forward.*

Open Nothing

The last group of people saying "Nothing" are experiencing something quite different. They may call it "empty" or "hollow." They may find it either exciting or frightening. This is a very creative "nothing" and a powerful place to be. One student called it "channeling"—a very apt description. Religious writings often describe the desire to empty oneself—hollow oneself out—become the void—open one's heart to God. Those who start from this place often do better acting than they've ever done before—more out-of-control (in a good way), and on the edge. Being able to experience true "nothingness" is wonderful. Meryl Streep calls it being "blank."

The important thing to understand about Being Present in the body is that there is *no wrong way to feel. It is all valid*—feeling powerful feelings, not feeling powerful feelings. It is even all right to feel blocked, stopped, trapped, numb, dead, tired—whatever. These are all okay places to begin.

MOTIVATION AND INSPIRATION

Tremendous energy potential for action is released when it is not wasted on resisting sensations. Suppression is tricky. You can be convinced that you're fine when you're really not. You feel "blah," "unmotivated," "unenthused." *That* is suppression. Count on it. Your natural state is full of feeling. Your natural state is Commitment.

There is no such thing as lack of motivation. Some people can go for a lifetime without being in touch with their commitments. They may even hate themselves for not being more pro-active in life. They try to motivate themselves. Their mothers and fathers try to motivate them. Everyone looks in the wrong direction. *It is natural to be motivated and enthused when you are fully present.* But if you are not fully present, you cannot be motivated. Motivation is *all* in the body.

AWARENESS OF THE NOW SURROUNDING THE BODY

Sometimes we are so unaware of what we are feeling that our only clue about what we are suppressing comes from what is happening around us—in our environment and in the dynamics of our lives. What we don't experience, we act out. Therefore, part of Being Present is being alert to what is actually going on in the world surrounding our bodies. There may be a startling contrast between what we think about ourselves and what the truth is.

George was about to do the first monologue in the first class after the summer break. He is a very powerful guy, full of passion.

Before he began, he laughed and said, "Boy, it seems like a long time since I've been in touch with what's going on in my body!" I told him to take his time. And as he stood there, I heard a great blaring of horns outside, apparently a traffic jam with angry drivers pounding on their horns. A new student turned to me and whispered, "Is it always like this?"

"Only for George," I whispered back. As he stood there getting in touch with the sensations in his body, the sounds became so loud that the class laughed. "Wow, George," I said out loud. "You must have a lot going on in your body."

He laughed and said, "You think so?" He felt angry about the horns blowing. He thought he was angry because of them. But when he began his monologue, it was clearly about a guy full of rage and frustration and sadness and passion. He rode the feelings beautifully.

After it was over, George calmed down as we talked about the effectiveness of what he did. Coincidentally, the horns calmed down along with him in a comically cosmic correlation.

It was by no means the only time I have observed the inner state mirrored by what is happening in the environment. Sometimes a student will resist or be upset by it instead of embracing it as George did.

One time a student was preparing to do a monologue. Downstairs a piano was playing with someone singing very loudly. He got more and more angered by it. How he felt about that piano was hilariously appropriate to the monologue he had chosen. Almost the moment he finished, the piano stopped. We all laughed.

BEING PRESENT TO WHAT-JUST-HAPPENED

There is a famous story about Laurence Olivier doing *Othello*. One night he gave a stunning performance—his best. He got standing ovations. After numerous curtain calls, he went storming to his dressing room and slammed the door. A friend followed him. "Larry, what's wrong? You were brilliant tonight."

"I know," he responded. "The problem is I don't know how I did it."

Being Present to What-Just-Happened is not an intellectual exercise. It is noticing—not figuring out. The mind has a tendency to attach old meanings and old patterns to events in the present.

That is unwise. It is important to notice What-Just-Happened—the actual facts, the actual dynamics—rather than make judgments about them.

A dear friend of mine would become upset when she experienced happiness. She'd have a great time and then wake up in the middle of the night in a panic. She was terrified of happiness, but she was unaware of this fear. Instead, she would be miserable, judge her life, call herself a failure, and feel "lost." When I first pointed out to her that she seemed to be having a reaction to a day of happiness, she called me crazy. "No! I *am* a failure!" Then she'd rattle off all the reasons that she thought she was a failure. Because we can prove almost any point of view, she would proceed to *prove* it to herself, if not to me.

It took some time and repeated episodes of happiness followed by panic for her to understand her pattern. It was confusing to her, because she *thought* she wanted happiness more than anything in the world, and she didn't notice that she had constructed her entire life in a way so that she didn't have to feel happy. Her job was so contrary to her whole nature that one might wonder how the hell she ever ended up in that line of work. However, because she needed or wanted to protect herself from the sensation of feeling happy, it was, indeed, perfect.

Once she was able to get through her panic to allow happiness, this dynamic dropped out of her life. She is no longer working in a law firm. She's doing work that expresses her being, and she is happy with feeling happy.

When I was first learning yoga, every pose brought up physical and emotional pain, because I was recovering from Lyme disease. After each pose, I found myself sobbing, "I can't do this!" I was convinced I should stop until I noticed that the thought came up immediately *after* I had actually done it! It was my mind's knee-jerk attempt to keep me safe from feeling good about myself.

There is tremendous power and potential for Breakthrough in simply noticing and stating the facts without judgment. Noticing What-Just-Happened, and seeing events for what they are without judgment, can spell the difference between success and failure.

LANDING

Because it is so important to notice What-Just-Happened, I always ask my students "Where did you Land?" after they complete monologues or scenes. They are always still feeling what their characters feel but they rarely know it. I sometimes forget, too, because what I think and feel seems so personal. That can be disturbing and dangerous to one's peace of mind and to one's relationships. Consciously Landing needs as much awareness as the landing in an actual airplane flight.

A goal I have for myself in plays, projects, and relationships is to be complete: fully expressed, have nothing left over, withhold nothing, and give all that I have to give. With certain roles, like Blanche DuBois in *A Streetcar Named Desire* or the woman in *Laughing Wild*, I used to feel like a clear, clean lake when it was all over. People would ask me how I could go through all that and be all right. They assumed I would be exhausted and drained. On the contrary, I felt clean because I had achieved full expression.

The roles taught me to want the same feeling in every endeavor and relationship. When I step over into the next realm, I want to be so expressed that I will have nothing left over. I want to feel like a clear, clean lake.

The need to Get Present and Land is not just a technique for acting, but also for life. If we all Got Present before an event, and Landed consciously afterwards, we would not drag our experiences through life like heavy loads that we dump into the next experience. Consciously taking time after working all day or going through a difficult experience allows us to be present for the next moment without bleeding all over the next people we encounter. What a gift to our friends and our loved ones not to drag them down with our unfelt feelings.

THE ABSOLUTE NOW

Strictly speaking, we can never be in the Absolute Now. The moment we acknowledge something, it is already changing. Being Present is messy and imperfect. We can only get close. The closer we get to being here and accepting where we are, the more joy we feel. It may be that only in the next life will we get to experience the ecstasy of being in the Absolute Now forever.

Meanwhile, it takes all our skill to stay as near the Now as possible, even though it is like trying to push repelling magnets together: the closer they get, the stronger the force to push away. Being as present as we can be in this life requires us to stay conscious moment by moment by moment, because the moment changes swiftly, wildly, or delicately. Being Present is the province of animals, babies, and the truly enlightened.

I vividly remember watching a baby's face one afternoon as he experienced being alive. I was fascinated by the speed at which life and sensation were happening to him. I could see it all in his face and body. He was so aware of all of the experiences—every sensation—every change of feeling flying over his expressions. He barely had time to experience and respond to one sensation before life thrust him on to the next. It was so fast it was breathtaking.

Sometimes Being Present in a day feels like walking through a storm that turns into a desert that turns into a field of daisies that turns into a dull, gray day that becomes a gorgeous sunset that becomes a rat-infested garbage dump that becomes a jungle of biting mosquitoes that becomes a dark, cool cave that turns into a warm bath, and so on. None of it seems connected, all random, good, bad, good, bad, bad, good, good, in no particular order that we can discern. As the baby did, our job is to hang in there with it and keep going.

A TRIGGER-HAPPY WORLD

Sometimes, when the eyes and ears of my soul are seeing and listening well, it seems that the entire world is in a conspiracy to help me feel what I need to feel. It is not comfortable. Sometimes it is plain awful. The world is full of triggers and button-pushers. It can feel as if the world is just an emotional mine field. But there are times when I really understand that what triggers me is a gift to help me to feel. I don't like it, but when I can take my feelings away from what or who has triggered me (not an easy task) and sit in my feelings and own my feelings without blaming or condemning the person or event, I can get down to what needs to be acknowledged. And when I do get down to the truth, the trigger releases, and I haven't shot anyone, even in my mind. I am even able to thank them in my heart.

At a performance of a comedy that I wrote and directed called *Intelejunt Dezyne*, a woman in the audience made a number of very loud comments during the welcome speech before the play. I was sitting behind the audience helpless to stop or control her. She not only disturbed the audience and the cast, she was sitting next to dear friends of mine. I was fit to be tied, as they say. And yeah, I wanted to kill her—not really, but you know the feeling. I worried that she would blurt out something during the show. She didn't but I did not enjoy the performance. I hated it. I even found myself angry at my cast if they forgot a line. I was triggered. Big time. Afterward, I heard a lot of agreeing comments about how awful she was and disturbing blah, blah, blah. One can always find agreement with how awful someone is. I went home, ate chocolate, and went to bed in a black mood. I woke up at four A.M. hating her and my play. Some part of me was sane enough to say, "Okay, Katherine. Let's just go into the feelings and take them away from her, from your play, from everything. These are your feelings." I started to become saner and not quite believe my negative thoughts, but I still felt awful.

Around seven A.M. I heard a friend who was staying with me shuffling around the kitchen making tea. I got up and asked her for help to get present with my difficult feelings. She's very committed to the process, so it was normal for us. The moment I focused on my body in her compassionate presence, I broke into wrenching sobs. I found the truth of what had really been triggered—how much had gone into the creation of my comedy about God: it was how much I cared about the world and how concerned I am about the difficulties we all face being human. Once I realized and acknowledged the depth of the feelings that had fueled my own creativity, I lightened up. That's what happens when we can actually get to the bottom of what has been triggered and face a truth. Soon the woman no longer bothered me. The next performance went well, and I was able to enjoy it. There were no problems.

How hard, hard, hard it is to get that triggers are there to point the way to what has not been felt and needs to be healed. Trying to fix what triggers intense emotions without feeling them and releasing the original pain is like driving the car hanging onto the dashboard instead of the wheel.

Triggers are gifts—sometimes very hard to accept, but there are so many of them out there—so many gifts for us all.

Actually, I have a name for that woman in the audience. No, it is not *that*. I call her a Pain Angel, someone who causes you pain and who forces you to do something or face something you have been avoiding or denying. It is not easy to call someone who causes you pain *an angel*, but it will release you from a lot of extended angst if you can see them as a gift. Start small. Start with people or things that may merely annoy you—like the woman in the audience—and gradually extend the agnomen to the boss who fires you, and to the spouse who leaves you. It is possible. And when you get a better job, and a happier marriage, or your peace as a single person, you may be able to look back and see them as Pain Angels. That is not easy, but then, none of this is.

THE GIFTS OF FEELING

In case you haven't noticed, the thing about Being Present is that there is *no wrong feeling*. I cannot overemphasize it: *There is no wrong feeling*. It is the most difficult thing for people to understand. No emotion is wrong. No sensation is wrong. Each real feeling gives us something we need. Fear is the doorway to great love. Rage can give us back our power. Grief can help us let go. Despair can transform us. Depression can strengthen us. Love opens our hearts. Unfortunately, too often we struggle against the experience—rather than *having* it—thereby missing the gift this feeling has for us.

We live in a society and were raised by parents who did not know how to be with their own emotions. Consequently, anything that a parent is unwilling to experience will be *felt* by the child, and yet *denied* to the child—especially fear and vulnerability. It takes a very self-accepting, emotionally available, and skilled parent to be able to help a child learn how to feel without acting out.

Body sensations are not judgmental. They just are.

Mastery is standing at the precise center of the body's sensations with a willingness to feel them as intensely and as long as they want to be there. Mastery is validating the sensations. Mastery is surrendering to the sensations. Mastery is looking for the gold in the images of sensations. Mastery is knowing that when feeling is fully experienced, energy for personal transformation and creativity is released and readily available. *Mastery is Being Present. Mastery is being alive and walking the path of one's heart's desires.*

FROM PAIN TO PEACE

There is a shift that I have noticed in my students and in myself that is quite remarkable. It is not a comfortable shift. It is when people become present enough with their pain and experience enough held-back feelings, that they begin to feel authentic peace, joy, love, and bliss. These feelings are unfamiliar for many of us. It is such unfamiliar territory that people will quite suddenly veer away from them back to the old, familiar pain. Believe it or not, familiar pain is more comfortable than unfamiliar joy.

When you become present enough to get to the experience of pure being and have the courage to stand in feelings, you will find that peace, joy, love, and bliss are the natural states of being.

Coming awake is an agony, but love awaits you. As you release the pain and cleanse your mind, as you dig through the dark earth of your being, you will encounter a great source of love and power within you. You will be able to unleash it as energy into the world.

Digging is hard. We must go into the dark places of our soul to find the veins of gold that are hidden there. It takes great effort and courage and support. And unlike the gold that we dig from beneath the earth, when you have truly gotten to the great love that is in your heart, you will discover that the more of it you use, the more you have.

The digging may look something like this: on the surface there is the crust, the deadness, a superficial layer that may even look good and feel fine. You may not want to spoil the tidy surface unless you realize that you need and want to get underneath it to be fulfilled.

So you dig and discover that even the initial digging will make you feel happy. You've started. You may think that you can stop there, that you've done enough. But you know that if you have not discovered great love, you need to dig more. So you continue.

Each limiting belief, each mass of withheld emotion and sensation will be difficult to uncover, but will bring a sense of satisfaction. You may hit a layer that looks impenetrable. "I *can't* get through this," you wail. Despair overcomes you. You feel overwhelmed. Life looks impossible. You sit in hopelessness. But if you do not run, suddenly, with great surprise and no effort, you discover you're through that layer and deeper in.

So, deeper you go, hopeful once more. And the boulders of deeply hidden beliefs are larger, harder to bring out to the light.

But you are stronger now. You believe in the work now. So you dynamite the obstacles with large blasts of emotion and truth. You're developing better tools and more skilled and skillful helpers. You can use truth like a laser now. But it is still hard going. Sometimes you think, "Will it never end? Is it worth all these tears and rage and fear and effort?"

Sometimes you think it isn't. Then you look around your life, and you see the healing and how much more love you have. So you continue more willingly, even more easily, knowing when to take breaks, and how to dig without forcing. Down deeper you go into your body, your mind, and your soul.

Then you sense that you are close to the source, because you suddenly feel the power deep within you. It is throbbing, wild, ready to explode. You know that all it needs is a small hole in the last layer, and it will gush out uncontrollably, splattering everyone and everything in its path. Now you may be terrified of it. The layer of terror that covers the great source shakes you to the core. Your mind goes wild. It is afraid. Your ego, your whole self-identity will be blasted apart if you uncover this energy.

"The power!" you say. "It is not me! I'm a reasonable, rational, cynical, functioning human being. I do my duty. I wash my clothes. I drive my car on the right side of the line. I am honest. I try to be good. I do my job. I take care of my responsibilities."

On and on your mind convinces you not to uncover all the love. It is terrified. Your body is terrified. For once they both agree. "Let's not do it," your body and mind say to each other. "Let's not go any further. Let's go back to the surface of life and cap the well. This could be dangerous."

So you may listen. You may cap the well. You may keep it capped for years. But you can't lie to yourself. You know it is there.

Eventually, you will go back. Somehow, with help, with the grace of God, you find the courage to touch your terror. And you touch it. You think you will die, and you are now willing to die, for death is preferable to the deadness that you feel at the surface when you are not connected to the source.

So you walk right up to the terror and into it. And you are surprised that it is easier to feel than to not feel. It may last only minutes—or days—or longer; but suddenly it is penetrated, and through the hole the love energy gushes forth.

You are stunned. It splashes on everyone and everything. The trees outside your house, your pets, the people you live with and see at the market. Everything gets splashed with it. You yourself are covered with it head to foot. And you laugh and laugh and find that you still have to wash your clothes and drive your car on the right side of the road. And you are grateful for the earthly activities that keep you from spinning off the planet. You feed the dog and fix the lamp and go to work, but, oh, with such a difference!

Fear and pain will appear now and then, yet more often you will cry with bliss, dance in the moonlight, laugh wildly, run in the rain with all your clothes on, and thank God for being truly alive at last.

FEAR OF HAVING LIFE BE GOOD

Here's a great question: How good are you willing to have life be? The fear of having life be good is very common. We all *think* we want our lives to be really good, but when good happens, we freak out. Many lottery winners have gone to pieces after winning big lotteries, because they can't take it. We all *think* we want to win the lottery, but the reality of it is quite another thing.

I know. Years ago I wrote a play called *Juno's Swans*, a comedy about sisters. My best friend read it, loved it, and wanted to play one of the sisters. We arranged to do a very small workshop production at the Ensemble Studio Theatre's sixth-floor experimental space. I was able to get a good director and cast.

We went into rehearsal and had great fun working on the play. It was the dead of winter. One day a blizzard nearly closed New York City. Our elevator even stopped working, but everyone slogged through the streets and climbed up the stairs to rehearse. I was deeply moved.

The first night of the workshop went so well that a few people came into the dressing room after the first act to tell us how much they liked it. Unheard of! "Can we just finish the play?" I pleaded.

After the play, a top-rate literary agent from William Morris Agency who had come that night, asked me to go out for a drink with him. He said he would like to represent me—which was also unheard of.

The next night, the people from the box office for the main stage came up and said there were many people getting out of limos wanting tickets for our play! My little play! I had no idea who they were! The next morning, the agent called and said that producers were interested in putting my play on Broadway, starring me and my best friend! Really mind-boggling!

It was all happening so fast—before we had even done three nights of a no-frills workshop of the play.

The agent started negotiating a contract, and that's when I panicked, but *I didn't know I was in a panic*. I somehow became enraged at the deal—balking at this and that. I said, "No!" The agent went back into negotiation with the producers, and I wish I didn't have to admit this, but I said no again. I remember being absolutely furious at the contract. In one embarrassingly synchronistic moment, I was walking down the street with my best friend, ranting on about this and that having to do with the contract and turned around only to run right into the producer.

The play did not get done on Broadway—ever. I screwed that one up royally because I was not present. I was unwilling to feel my fear. I had no idea I was afraid. I had turned it into righteousness and rage. (So like one of the characters in my play, unfortunately.) I wish I had had someone somewhere who might have asked me, "Katherine, what's going on in your body right now?" I didn't. How good was I willing for my life to be? Not very much, unfortunately.

Well. At least that story has turned into a good teaching tool.

A woman comes to class. She looks terrible. Her skin is gray. I'm shocked. She gets up to work. "Before I get present, I just have to tell y'all something." Oh, my God, I'm thinking. She's going to tell us that she's got cancer, and she's dying! I'm about to burst into tears. "I've got five gigs lined up for my band."

I'm not sure I'm hearing correctly. Isn't that a good thing? "What?" I ask confused.

"Five gigs." She whispers, "Five really well-paying gigs. They came in today."

Oh. I get it. She's freaked. She's won the lottery. An impossible dream has become a reality. Fortunately, she gets present and experiences her fear. She cries, shakes, and then continues to move forward.

Since that day, she has confronted her fear of having things be good and continues to move steadily forward along her path. She's got a great CD, an active web site, a side business, and she's flying back and forth to London to appear on television there, making more money than she ever thought possible. She continues to be afraid. She continues to shake, but now she gets that "a whole lotta shakin' goin' on" is just part of moving forward. Shaking and trembling are what students often do when they are about to do Breakthrough work. Teeth chatter, legs shake, or they feel an invisible trembling. They remind me of the early religious sect called the Shakers who shake when they feel close to God.

I have observed over and over again the tremendous fear we have of having things be really good—better than we have ever known. Peace, joy, bliss, happiness are truly unfamiliar territory to most of us. At first we assume that something is wrong or certainly *will* go wrong very shortly. Dustin Hoffman accepts an Academy Award wondering when he is going to get polio.

How good are you willing to have it be?

Are you willing for it to be deeply good, peacefully good?

Are you willing for it to be not just pleasure and fun and excitement, but *good*?

BENEFITS OF BEING PRESENT

The other night a man who has been in my class for years was getting present and squirming. "I don't want to go there," he said suddenly. He became upset and frustrated. "I don't want to feel this. I hate this. Why do I have to be present, for God's sake!? Why do I have to feel this? Why would anyone want to feel this? What good does it do?"

Those are good questions.

Frankly, most of us would rather do *anything* than actually be in our bodies. We choose to overeat, overwork, drink, do drugs, shop, watch TV, play Spider Solitaire, surf the web for hours, and indulge any number of addictions, rather than actually be here. Being here, being a human being in a human body is *hard*. We will never be perfect at it.

Over the years, I have come to realize more and more how important it is to become as present as possible. I believe that if you really want to contribute to the world, you will dedicate your life to self-responsibility and owning what you feel rather than projecting it all over everyone around you. Your greatest present to the world is to *Be Present*. If you do nothing else in your life, this will be your gift, because how you affect everyone you touch affects everyone *they* touch. A virus can spread throughout the world in twelve days—so can ideas and actions. Being Present, committing, and communicating impacts everyone and everything.

Sometimes it is terribly difficult and painful to be present. So, you should know that there are great rewards to it. When you are present:

1. You know what you want.

2. You are clearer about what the next steps are—even tiny steps.

3. You are more in touch with what is called intuition.

4. You are more responsive to the outside world—to signals, to signs, and to suggestions from the Universe. They're there all the time. It is only when you're present that you notice them.

5. You are more compassionate.

6. You are more creative.

7. You are easier to be with and work with.

8. You make fewer mistakes.

9. You will be healthier physically, emotionally, and mentally.

10. You know what your true commitments are.

11. You will be sexier. No kidding.

There was a girl in class who got up to work. She felt awful. She looked kinda awful. But as she allowed herself to really feel what was going on in her body, she became more sensual and appealing. She said that she felt fat like a cow. I told her to really allow herself to feel fat like a cow, to surrender her body to the feeling. She slumped down and described how sluggish and fat and sullen and swollen she felt. In contrast to her words, she became sexier. I have seen it happen to people over and over again as they consciously experience even very uncomfortable physical sensations. So, at the very least, you wanna be sexy? Be Present.

Probably the most important reason to be present is so you can be free—free to act, free to be, free to say no when you want to, free to say yes when you want to, free to choose, free to create your life, free from the pain of your past, free from the fear of the future, free to go forward, free to be alone, free to be in your power and use it for yourself, free to be with someone, free to have fun, free from addictions, free to live and be fully alive—free to love and follow your heart's desires. If you can Be Present, you are free. You are free to follow your heart's desires.

SUMMARY

Being Present is about being in your body. One question is all you need: *What sensation am I experiencing in my body right now?*

I have found that the most effective way to get present is with a partner, a Compassionate Witness—someone who can help you be with your sensations without having to fix, change, heal, or alter your experience in any way. This Compassionate Witness process is outlined toward the end of the book. If you want to skip to that chapter and set in motion that experience now, do so. Meanwhile, do what you can to be your own Compassionate Witness and separate your thoughts from upsetting emotions by going directly to the sensations in your body.

RELAXATION

Relaxation is the secret of all good acting.
　　　　　　　　　　—John Gielgud

elaxation is, in its own way, the first principle. I sometimes call it the last-to-get-the-first-to-go principle. Let a little fear slip in the door, and Relaxation tends to leap out the window. Relaxation begins with *willingness*. One must be *willing* to let go. One must be *willing* to stop trying to control everything. One must be *willing* to feel. One must be *willing* to communicate. One must be *willing* to tell the truth. Nothing can begin or move without at least a drop of willingness. Willfulness is antithetical to Relaxation. Because one must be willing, Relaxation could be definitely considered the first principle.

When the need for Relaxation in acting is understood, it takes on the quality of being all important—as do Commitment and Being Present and Communication. Relaxation and brilliance are in direct correlation. It is the one visible difference between the inexperienced actor and the accomplished one. I cannot think of an actor or a person I admire who is not relaxed. In almost every actor's autobiography there is a significant moment in which the actor describes discovering the importance of Relaxation.

John Gielgud in *Early Stages* writes, "I suppose the truth of the matter was that I was relaxed for the first time. The finest producers I have worked with since have told me that this relaxation is the secret of all good acting, but we were never taught it at the dramatic schools. One's instinct in trying to work oneself into an emotional state is to tighten up. When one is young and nervous, one tightens the moment one attempts to act at all, and this violent tension, if it is passionately sincere, can sometimes be effective on the stage. But it is utterly exhausting to the actor and only impresses the audience for a very short space of time."

It is just as true in life. The more powerful in terms of leadership a person is, the more relaxed he appears. Think of Mahatma Gandhi or the Dalai Lama. Gurus walk slowly and peacefully.

How important is genuine Relaxation? It is absolutely essential to moving along your path. If there is no Relaxation, nothing moves. Nothing. Things become constipated, stopped, and stuck. In order to move forward toward your heart's desires, there must be some measure of Relaxation. The less Relaxation there is, the slower the movement. The more Relaxation there is, the faster things can move.

It is hard to move through physical and spiritual gravity. A commitment that is heavy is hard to keep afloat. It becomes very difficult for actors to maintain a sense of lightness when trying to create a career. It requires enormous personal mastery not to make each audition, each job, each opening night *important* and *significant*. When you play a high-stakes game that is based on a true commitment, it is imperative to be relaxed.

Many people seek to develop Relaxation through religion, meditation, yoga, creative visualization, positive thinking, and hypnosis—any practice that calms and trains the mind. Each is fine, but if you use them or any type of mind control as a way to avoid *feeling your feelings*, you are being counterproductive to your own movement forward, and you will never achieve true Relaxation. We've all known people who talk a good game, but play it in a very different way. The spiritual hypocrite is someone who is not really present.

Because Relaxation is characteristic of the powerful, teenagers sense it. It is why it is so important to teens to look cool. But looking cool is false Relaxation based on suppressing feelings and not caring about anything (or pretending not to care about anything). Relaxation for the sake of Relaxation is not it. Like the other principles, Relaxation does not stand alone—not if you want to do anything that is meaningful to you.

It is one thing to be relaxed on vacation, at an ashram, or hanging out in your apartment. It is another to be relaxed while pursuing something you love, need, and want. The more passionate and heartfelt the Commitment, the greater the need for Relaxation. The aim is to be fully committed *and* relaxed. Commitment and Relaxation are not opposed; they work together.

Most people do not give Relaxation the importance it deserves—especially in America. Keeping your nose to the grindstone may just wear down your nose. Commitments do require effort, and the reason people rehearse a play or practice diligently at a sport is to achieve the Relaxation that is so necessary to mastery.

Relaxation seems like a luxury. Most of us are afraid of the word *luxury*—taking luxurious baths, spending an hour watching birds at a feeder, enjoying the play of sun in the trees, or lying in bed listening to the rain. Creativity is a luxury. It is a luxury of the spirit and the mind and the body. How luxury refreshes the spirit and body!

WHAT IS RELAXATION?

Being Present is about the body. Relaxation is about the mind. It is about the thoughts that increase tension or create Relaxation. While Relaxation may show up as apparent physical ease, it is a result of thought—of context. It has been said that context is everything. Indeed, if you approach any situation with a negative or heavy context, it will be nearly impossible to relax.

According to Webster, *to relax* means "1: to make less tense or rigid: slacken, 2: to make less severe or stringent, 3: to make soft or enervated, 4: to relieve from nervous tension...to cast off social restraint, nervous tension, or attitude of anxiety or suspicion...to relieve constipation." Yes. To relax is to let go and let flow. So, Relaxation is about creating movement—which is the purpose of this book.

There is no definition for actually *being relaxed*. The characteristics of *being relaxed* are: willingness, acceptance, ease, lightness, surrender, humor, self-confidence, playfulness, trust, and faith. The opposite of Relaxation is heaviness, weightiness, seriousness, resistance, significance, rigidity, negative thinking, holding on, willfulness, worry, tension, and gravity.

In order to truly get the importance of Relaxation, let's look at what gets in the way of Relaxation and how damaging it can be: addiction, conflict, dishonesty, distraction, comparison, doubt, expectation, procrastination, perfectionism, denial, righteousness, considerations, cynicism, obsession, and all negative mind-sets are the opposite of Relaxation. They are crippling to artists and anyone pursuing a dream.

NEGATIVE JUDGMENT

Negative judgment is powerful. Harsh criticism can stop us dead in our tracks. It can prevent us from moving forward toward our hearts' desires. When negative judgment manifests as self-criticism, it is killing. "This is awful." "I'm terrible." "Who do I think I am?" "I'm not good enough." "I'll never be good enough." Tragically, if we believe such thoughts, our creativity dies.

We all know horror stories about authority figures who harshly judged their charges, effectively cutting them off from pursuing their talents: a left-handed student is forced to write with her right hand, which suffocates her creative writing; or a trombone player is humiliated by a band leader and never plays trombone again. Do you have such a story?

Negative criticism when we are vulnerable can turn us into creative invalids.

According to Webster, *invalid* means "to make sickly or disabled" and "to remove from active duty." *To invalidate* means "to weaken or destroy the cogency." Invalidation is deadly. It is disempowering and enervating. Lying, withholding the truth, being secretive, isolating, abandoning, ignoring, not really listening, complaining, and shaming are forms of invalidation along with any form of abuse, physical, mental, or emotional. As a technique in self-improvement, invalidation and criticism are crashing failures. They do not work to help you or anyone further along their paths. Invalidation is poisonous. It makes one sickly. It turns one into an invalid. I tell my students that if criticizing them actually helped, I would use it. But it doesn't. I'm only interested in what works.

George Bernard Shaw said in *The Art of Rehearsal*, a small pamphlet he wrote for directors, "Don't criticize. If a thing is wrong and you don't know exactly how to set it right, say nothing. It discourages and maddens an actor to be told merely that you are dissatisfied...if you get angry and complain...you will destroy the whole atmosphere in which art breathes." Shaw's advice holds true in all aspects of life.

Lest one think that negative judgment and invalidation are harmful only to the young, the weak, the sensitive, the unrealized, let me cite some examples of extraordinary talent wounded by invalidation.

David Lean, who directed the seminal motion picture *Lawrence of Arabia*, stated in a documentary, "I find it very difficult directing movies. One's awfully easily shaken, you know." He then described going to a critics' luncheon at the Algonquin Hotel in New York in 1970. He had expected to be honored and feted. Instead, he was roundly criticized for directing *Ryan's Daughter*. He was so devastated that he lost any desire to direct for three years.

The power of invalidation is particularly devastating when something—an idea, a creation—is embryonic or new-born. A twenty-four-year-old astrophysicist, Subrahmanyan Chandrasekhar, was presented by his mentor, Arthur Eddington, at a prestigious meeting of the Royal Astronomical Society in 1935. At the meeting, Chandrasekhar spoke about his theory of black holes. After he spoke, his mentor blasted him and his theory. Chandrasekhar abandoned his work with black holes for almost forty years. Fortunately, eventually Chandraskehar returned to his work. So important was Chandrasekhar's once-ridiculed theory that he would be awarded a Nobel Prize for it in 1983.

Stephen Sondheim, who infused new life into musical theater with his many ground-breaking creations, said in an interview in *TheaterWeek* (June 8, 1992), "I know how hurt I am when some of those people trash me in public...I will not do that to anybody unless they're dead...somebody who I think is rotten can say something rotten about me, and I'm still hurt. Everybody should support everybody."

I would venture to say that you are probably no more immune to criticism and invalidation than Lean, Chandrasekhar, or Sondheim.

THE PURPOSE OF NEGATIVE THINKING

Negative thinking and self-criticism are so deeply embedded in our minds that they have the status of addiction. Therefore it is important to understand why they exist. Essentially, it is about protection. The mind is terrified of intense feeling, so it engages all its resources to stop any forward movement that causes out-of-the-ordinary sensation. All too often it works. The mind wants to protect us from anything it perceives as dangerous. Therefore, the feelings around fear trigger negative thoughts.

The automatic, negative mind is like a terribly fearful, over-protective parent who is concerned only about the physical safety of the child. Negative thinking is so difficult to deal with because often it started with those we love and who love us most profoundly: our parents. Rejecting negative thinking is like rejecting someone who is trying to protect you.

The negative mind needs reassurance rather than rejection. Be kind to it. Be gentle. It is afraid for you. Unfortunately, the closer one gets to what one truly wants the greater the fear. Consequently, the negative judgment gets louder, and the mind will use whatever ammunition it can find to get us to *stop* the closer we get to realizing our hearts' desires.

Have you tried to help a friend who is mired in self-hatred and self-judgment? Impossible. It is even worse when you're trying to deal with yourself.

So, what can you do when the negative thinking is raging out-of-control and you believe it? What do you do when your mind tells you you're too fat or old or stupid or not good enough to do what you want to do, and you have bought it hook, line, and sinker? Remember: *there is no arguing with the mind when it is dedicated to negative thinking.*

GO TO THE SOURCE

The most effective way to deal with negativity is to take the focus away from the mind and go directly to the *unfelt feelings* that cause it. Get Present. Don't try to talk yourself out of any thought.

The mind cannot deal with the mind when it is convinced. It is a losing battle. Trying to protect the body from doing anything that will cause intense feelings, the mind will come up with every thought—everything it can—in its assumed survival battle. It will lie to us—and often does—just to get us to stop whatever we are doing that is causing the body to feel.

The actors and writers in my classes have powerful minds— very creative. I don't even attempt to deal with their minds when the negativity comes gushing up. Every time an actor takes a risk creatively and starts to feel fear, the mind kicks in to stop the person from doing whatever they are doing that is creating the fear. People so want to cling to the negative thinking and believe it. If they believe it, they don't have to move forward. Then they won't have to feel. Oh, God, don't let me do the most fearful thing! Don't let me move toward my heart's desire!

Any unfelt feeling is a trigger for negativity to the mind. A particularly bright student of mine automatically drew negative decisions and conclusions about herself, her life, her talent— everything—constantly. She was so quick. The mind is fast on the draw when it comes to shooting us down. However, every time she came to class and allowed herself to feel the feelings of sadness and fear that she had been suppressing, she would do excellent work. Afterward, her extreme negativity would calm down—for a while. Gradually, the more present she becomes, the fewer negative thoughts and conclusions she makes about herself. They are now even a source of amusement because every single one of them has been proven wrong. "I'm slow as an actress," she said to me recently.

"I don't think so," I said.

"Oh, yes," she insisted. "I need a lot of time to rehearse." A few days later, she was called suddenly to replace an actress in an Off Broadway show. She went on with about three day's rehearsal and was very successful. No problem.

"Slow, eh?" I teased her a week or so later. We laughed. God does have a sense of humor.

I feel as if I'm bronco riding sometimes when I teach. It is a challenge to get people to accept what they feel. They *want* to stay in the mind. As negative as it is, it feels safer there. I'm not trying to suppress the mind. I'm trying to bypass the fear that it is reacting to and to go to the source of this negativity. So I ask the dreaded question, "What's going on in your body?" If I can get people through I-don't-want-to-do-this to what they are actually feeling, we're off and running. If I can help a person to feel their fear and do it anyway—like the good book title urges—the negativity calms down. It always does. So it becomes obvious that *negative thinking is not about the truth: It is about unfelt feeling.*

THE COMMITTEE

Think of your negative mind as an advertising committee whose purpose is to keep you safe and who go to work when you step outside the comfort zone. They meet in the board room and come up with the thought or thoughts that you will believe so you will stop whatever it is that you are doing that brings up extraordinary feelings. If you buy what they come up with, they can go hang out at the cooler and chat. If you press forward again, they rush to the board room and brain-storm more ideas until they come up with the thoughts that will effectively stop you and bring you back once more into that narrow, safe corridor of experience.

Be aware that the automatic, negative mind is not stupid—not at all. It uses our intelligence against us. The better our minds are, the better they are in devising negative thinking that seems indisputable.

Sometimes you are on your path, and the committee will try to paint horrifying pictures of the future—perhaps hoping that you'll quit whatever it is you are doing that is bringing up such intense feeling. You can trick it by letting it say the worst and keep moving anyway. The one mental response that pulls the rugs out from under the committee's chairs is, "So what?"

One time I was asked to perform the one-woman play *The Search for Signs of Intelligent Life in the Universe* by Jane Wagner. The incomparable Lily Tomlin had performed it on Broadway. I had seen her performance and was in awe of her. The play is nearly three hours long with fourteen different characters, and I had less than a month to learn it before performing it in a five-hundred-seat theater.

I accepted the challenge to do it because I *loved* the piece in spite of my fear and the obstacles. However, I would wake up in the middle of the night in a full-body sweat thinking, "Oh, my God. I'm not going to remember all those lines! I'll be awful. The audiences will be so upset that I'm not Lily Tomlin that they'll walk out! I don't have the physical strength to do it. *I will die if I do this.*" I could argue with none of these thoughts as I lay there, heart pounding, gasping for breath. The only way out of my terror was to say, "Okay. So what?" to every thought the committee came up with. Death was a big one, but as I lay there, I even wrote a lovely obituary for myself, "E. Katherine Kerr died on stage last night while performing...uh...*beautifully* performing...etc." As I accepted the fact that I might, indeed, die, the committee was struck dumb, and I calmed down and went back to sleep. I got through the show fine.

Another time, I went to the first rehearsal of a play. The rest of the cast had done many readings of the play. I was new. They were wonderful in the rehearsal. I was not. In fact, my committee came up with the judgment, "You're going to stink in this." After the rehearsal, everyone left, and I sank onto the floor. My heart was pounding. I felt humiliated and sick to my stomach. I wanted to quit. That made the committee happy until I said, "So what if I stink? The people who love me will continue to love me, and the ones who don't will be really happy." I relaxed, and I was fine in the show. "So what?" can be a powerful response if you really mean it.

Negative thinking burns itself out when it learns that it is not going to stop us. It has a flame-out. Flame-outs happen in nature all the time. Just before something dies, it has a burst of life: a match, the fall colors, or the miraculous period just before someone dies when a person seems suddenly much better. So it is with negative thinking and negative patterns just before they leave us. The louder the mind screams, the more it is defending its territory because it is losing the war with our hearts. Eventually the committee will quit and be replaced by an inner voice that is encouraging, compassionate, and wise.

THOUGHT LOGS

Because most often the basis of negative judgment is unfelt fear, we need to learn how to sit with fear without drawing negative conclusions and decisions about ourselves and our lives. Unfortunately, when we don't know how to sit with fear, we seem *compelled* to feed it. We attach all kinds of wild, irrational thoughts to it. Being with fear can be likened to sitting in front of a fire. We can learn to be with it and watch it burn, or we can feed it with what I call Thought Logs. Thought Logs are negative thoughts such as "I'm going to fail," "I can't do this," or "I'm not good enough." We throw each one of these thoughts onto the fire of our fear until the fire rages out of control, leaving our hearts' desires in ashes.

Notice that when you feel afraid, you may be, in reality, sitting at home in front of a fire. Nothing is wrong. Remember: *fear is all about the future.* Don't pick up Thought Logs and throw them on the fire. Commit to five minutes of not picking up any more Thought Logs about the future. Put them down. Watch and feel the fire as pure sensation until it dies down—and it will. Then your mind will be clear enough to see options, and you can think more effectively. You will save a lot of energy.

It is the same process with anger. Anger is very difficult to just feel without attaching it to someone or something. There's a joke about the guy who goes to borrow his neighbor's lawn mower. He's afraid to ask to borrow it. In his mind he makes up all the things his neighbor is going to say to him. Because he has listened to and believed all the negative things he himself made up in his head, by the time he rings the bell and the neighbor answers all he can say is, "Screw you and your lawn mower!"

When you are very angry and afraid, take at least five minutes and just sit with the feelings of anger and fear. Every time a feeling wants to attach to a person, place, or thing that triggered it, take psychic scissors and snip the energy tendrils. Don't let a feeling attach to thoughts in your mind. The reason to prevent attachment is that attachment prolongs and increases your discomfort.

Think of your anger as your energy. The power that is in anger will not be yours to use until you *own* it. *As long as you attach and attribute your anger to someone else, it is not available for you to use. It is theirs. You have given away your power to that person.*

Until you learn to own anger and use it well, you will have many people and situations that will keep triggering your rage. Do you have that in your life? Is your rage triggered easily? Then you might want to take a look at how you are not taking care of yourself.

I once asked a friend who had conversations with God before a book by that name was written, "How do I handle my resentment toward my mother? She won't communicate with me about anything, so I feel stuck in my anger toward her." The answer surprised me. "Empower yourself, and you will see your resentments simply melt away." And that is exactly what happened over the years. As I gave myself what I needed and wanted, I no longer resented her for not giving them to me as a child. I was using my anger/power for myself.

NEGATIVE JUDGMENT EXERCISE

Once you begin to question your negative self-judgments, you will begin to see another truth about them: *they are lies.* They are not merely lies; they take what is best about us and twist it into something negative. Until one is more present, the fact that our negative judgments are lies is difficult to see. We hold old, negative self-judgments about ourselves to be true. However, we need to upgrade our self-advertisements.

In my workshop I teach an exercise that is always very powerful and illustrates this undeniably. If you have any difficulty with negative self-judgment, it would benefit you a great deal to do the exercise. Perform it in a group if possible:

1. Get two blank sheets of paper. On one piece of paper, write down all the negative judgments and considerations about why you cannot have what you want, do what you want, or be what you want to be. Write them all down—every secret, deep, ugly thought.

2. When you have finished with the first paper, on the second piece of paper, as an exercise (you don't have to believe any of it) reverse each judgment 180 degrees. Rewrite each judgment in the most positive way possible. For example, if you wrote "I'm not really good with people" on the first piece of paper, then write "I'm really good with people" on the second page. Once you complete that, title it *This Is Who I Really Am.* Do not even allow the negative judgments air time.

3. Now, read aloud *only* the positive statements to the group or to a friend. Read each statement out loud clearly and communicate it like you mean it! Look people right in the eye—looking people right in the eye is a requirement—and speak with gusto. Pretend, if you must in order to do it. You may squirm and feel very embarrassed. You may cry. Stop and get present with your feelings if you need to do so,

and then press on with conviction. Have fun. Pause after each statement, and let people applaud or comment. You may not get it in regard to yourself, but you will see it with everyone else in the group—that what they think is a lie is actually the real truth about who they are.

4. Take the piece of paper with the negative judgments and tear it up into tiny pieces. If you are able to do so safely, you may even burn it ritualistically.

5. Now, retype and print the statements entitled *This Is Who I Am*. Put them up where you can see them and read them every day until you get it.

This little exercise can help you to redo your old, incorrect, keep-yourself-safe advertising. This little exercise can blow your mind. It will help you let go of the lies you tell yourself to stay safe.

GUILT AND SHAME

Guilt and shame are like psychic glue. You will not move at all if you are stuck in guilt and shame. In fact, if you feel bad and wrong about something, you may never be able to let it go or stop doing it. You may *control* it, or try to control it, but you won't make essential changes.

Slap shame and guilt on the behavior you want to change, and it is like putting mortar on bricks. You are walled in. There is no escape. There is rage in guilt. If you feel guilty for overeating, you will use the rage in your guilt to punish yourself by continuing to overeat. If you feel guilty about your behavior toward someone, eventually you will find a reason to be angry at them and end the relationship. If you feel guilty about smoking, it will be all the more difficult to stop smoking. You will actually punish yourself by continuing the very behavior you want to stop.

All religions recognize the rage in guilt and shame. It is why forgiveness is the foundation of redemption. Getting rid of guilt is no easy task if you have convinced yourself about how wrong you are. "What a jerk I am," "I hate myself," etc. You're stuck. Instead, practice self-forgiveness.

ADDICTIONS

Addictions will allow you to keep moving—in the wrong direction—down the tubes. Addictions cloud or soften an uncomfortable experience in order to make it bearable, but they do so only momentarily. It does not last. Anyone who gives up any addiction must come face-to-face with the pain that the addiction has disguised. If you cannot be in your body because you are altering and drugging it with booze, drugs, food, cigarettes, or sex, you might be able to hang in there for the short run, but you will not make it over the long haul.

A professional career in theater and film is a kind of crucible that makes us or breaks us. It is a sink-or-swim, live-or-die kind of life. Those who die because they have fallen prey to alcohol and drugs, like Marilyn Monroe, John Belushi, Heath Ledger, Philip Seymour Hoffman, or a long list of stars, are sad examples of it.

I used to be addicted to cigarettes. June Havoc, who directed me as Blanche in *A Streetcar Named Desire*, said in her emphatic way, "Katherine! Your body is your temple! It is all you have! You must stop smoking!" She was nothing if not dramatic! Miraculously, I took her advice. It was one of the hardest things I've ever done, but I did stop smoking. Underneath the addiction to cigarettes was a lot of pent-up anger—and power. Cigarettes turn our real fire into smoke. Do you want to just smoke, or do you want to be on fire with the passion of your heart's desires?

OBSESSIONS AND CONFLICTS

The mind has many devices to try to stop you from pursuing your heart's desires. Obsessions and conflicts turn us into little rats running around in circles rather than moving forward.

How many times have you listened to friends obsessing about something? They talk and talk and talk and talk about it. They get stuck in the story. The story about it is endless. Nothing you can say alleviates their torment. No advice works.

Eventually you want to strangle them, or go away, or scream, "Shut up! I can't listen to the story any more!"

It is evident that they are not going to get anywhere thinking and talking about the problem—just like my friend Betty after her cancer operation, obsessing about her boyfriend when the real problem was her terror of cancer. It was easier for her to talk about her boyfriend—endlessly.

Whatever a person is obsessing about is not the problem. If they can focus for a moment on actually feeling, the real problem will emerge.

Another dear friend named Viv fell into a totally addictive love affair around the same time her friend Betty died. She was so wrapped up in the affair that she confessed she felt nothing about Betty's death. In fact, Viv was wildly happy—while her addiction was being satisfied. She spent most of her time calling her lover in London from Los Angeles, talking for hours on the telephone. Soon she made the trip to England, and predictably, the affair crashed and she was crushed.

On her return, we had dinner together. She was smoking a lot and barely able to maintain eye contact. The story about this affair was going on and on. As gently as I could I asked, "Viv, what's going on in your body, right now?"

Immediately, probably because she was so exhausted from keeping up her obsession, she felt a crushing weight on her heart. Tears gushed forth. She was so grief-stricken she could barely sit in her chair. Her obsession was gone. She stopped talking about her affair. Instead, she spoke of all the losses she had experienced in the last several years—many dear friends who died of AIDS and then, Betty. She had believed she would die if she allowed herself to experience her grief and what was going on in her body. Being afraid of dying from feeling is a common fear. Of course she didn't die. What a relief it was to be with her while she grieved. She was real again.

THE ENDLESS STORY

Addictions are not just physical. There are mental addictions. We can get stuck in our stories and endless dramas. People who experience real tragedies and have some measure of health will do everything they can to get through them. People who are using their stories and dramas to not be present will refer to them at every opportunity.

Drama queens or kings get stuck in their endless story. A student comes back to class after having been away doing a show. The show actually was quite successful for her, but she's determined to tell us how awful the other actors in the show were. I had already heard the story, but when I ask her what's going on in her body, she dodges the question and starts on a rampage—how much she hated them, wants to kill them. Her hatred is building, and she's not getting anywhere. I ask her to start her piece from where she is. "I don't know what I want to do," she growls, her face all twisted in fury. Once more it is confirmed that until you're present, you don't know what you want to do.

"Tell me what to do," she demands. I don't. I ask her again what's going on in her body. She won't go there. She stays in her story about the people, the injustice, blah, blah, blah. She has a firm grip on the Pain of the Past. Not present. Not relaxed. She's having a tantrum. She's being a determined victim. She really wants to go on and on and tell us everything that happened.

I start bronco riding. I keep asking her what is going on in her body *right now*.

"I hate them," she says. "I hate them" is a negative thought, not what's in her body, obviously.

"Where do you feel that?" I persist.

"In my face," she says. We're getting somewhere now.

"Would you be willing to feel the feelings for eight seconds?" I ask. She nods slightly, lips pinched tightly together. "Okay. Here we go. One! Don't attach what you're feeling to those people. Two. Take scissors and snip those energy tendrils that want to attach what you're feeling to them. Three. Stay here. Four. You're doing great. Five. Bring your mind back to right here! Six. Feel all that fury and power in your body. Now, for two counts—just two counts really feel what you're feeling, and *own it!* Seven. Eight. Great. You stayed on the bull for eight seconds, and you didn't lose your hat!" (Nor did I as her teacher.) "Are you present now?"

"Yeah," she says a bit begrudgingly. Then more softly, "I want to sing a song from the show." Now she's present. She knows what she wants to do. I notice that. She doesn't. She sings a song and does two monologues from the show that she was in. She does them brilliantly.

Why was she clinging so ferociously to the Pain of the Past and to the story around it? Perhaps, being here, in the emptiness that an actor faces every time a job ends, was too frightening for her. It is easier to go to the Pain of the Past or the Fear of the Future than to the Void of the Present.

Afterward, another student tells her that he thinks she may be the best actress he has ever seen. She's transforming herself from a drama queen into a queen of drama.

It is very difficult to be around complainers who can be so right about how wrong everything in life is. However, after listening to people complain about their life, the listener feels dumped on and is left feeling debilitated. Unfortunately, complainers seem tireless. Complaining is a way people have of not actually being present with what they are feeling.

Pain can be so attractive, so familiar, so easy to hide in. Pain and negative thinking can be so compulsive. Be a creative alchemist instead: *turn your pain into gold. Create something.*

TRYING

Once people understand the importance of Relaxation, they often *try* to relax. While Relaxation is the goal, forced Relaxation is not the path. How many times have you heard someone said, "Don't be afraid. Relax! You'll be fine!" It rarely helps. "Relax! Hey! Loosen up!" Maybe it works for a moment. Then, you're suddenly all knots again. The tension won't go away. You know you should relax. So you keep trying. "I'm trying! I'm trying!" you wail.

Years ago, an inexperienced director kept hounding me for "more energy." In my own lack of experience I responded by *trying* to be energetic. Instead of relaxing, I became tense, wooden, and utterly exhausted. Naturally, the director was unsatisfied and kept saying *"More* energy—not *less!"*

Finally, one day I was so tired and upset I thought, "Hell with it. Let him fire me," and I stopped trying. I gave up and stopped pushing for energy. I relaxed. I was certain I was doing exactly the opposite of what the director wanted, but I no longer was trying to please him; and I started to have fun in the rehearsal. It was my last day anyway, I thought.

"That's what I wanted!" the director shouted after the scene. I was amazed, and I took note that henceforth whenever anyone would ask me for "more energy," I would translate it into *Let go.* With experience, and as I learned how to relax, directors have stopped asking me for more "energy." Being relaxed does not mean having no energy—quite the opposite, in fact.

Don't try to relax. Eliminate *trying*. Eliminate the very word *trying* as much as possible. *Trying* actually means *struggling*. A stage hypnotist who wants to ensure that the subject does *not* perform the requested action asks the subject *to try*. That guarantees the subject will provide hilarious struggle for the audience. "*Try* to get up from the chair." The subject is glued and can't stand up. "Come on!" The hypnotist urges. "You're not *trying* hard enough! Try harder!" So, the subject struggles harder and harder. Red in the face. Battling the chair. The audience laughs and laughs.

Please have Relaxation be your intention, which is important, but do not *try*. As the hypnotist demonstrates, trying to be or do anything practically guarantees it won't happen. A friend once said, "I've been trying all my life to be who I already am." She was exhausted from the effort.

WHY

We try so hard to figure out why we're feeling what we're feeling in order to not have to feel. Why?! Why am I feeling so sad? Why am I so scared? Much of the time it really doesn't matter *why* we feel what we feel. We just need to feel it. Often we think we're wrong to feel what we feel, so we want to think our way out of it.

The truth is we may not really know the causes of our feelings. There are many triggers. But the causes? Who knows, really? Chemical? Childhood pain? Past lives? Maybe emotions are like the weather, and some of us live in a highly variable climate like New England, or a hot one like the tropics. Do we try to resist the weather? Wouldn't that be silly? Perhaps it is just as futile to resist our sensations and emotions. The more freely they flow through us unimpeded, the less damage they leave. Damned up emotions tend to act like extreme weather, flooding or burning everything in their path when they finally come out.

When we really allow ourselves to feel what we're feeling, we may discover some deeper cause than we supposed. A woman phones me. She's afraid that she may not love her boyfriend. She gets present. She discovers she's really scared. After being with her fear for a while, she realizes that things are so good in her life right now that *that* is what scares her most. She says that her boyfriend is the greatest guy she has ever known—very unlike anyone else—totally unexpected—not like any of her fantasies—but a great guy.

The cause of her feelings was something quite different than she thought.

Asking "Why?" before we are present, just means "I don't like." I don't like feeling angry, sad, scared.

TRYING TO THINK POSITIVELY

There is help for negative thinking—but it is not *trying* to think positive thoughts in the midst of intense emotional upset. If someone having dark, negative thoughts is told to be grateful and thank God for the good things, that probably will make them feel worse. Positive thinking does not work for dedicated negative thinkers. I know. I was one.

A friend often tried to help me with some positive thinking when I was in the middle of deep self-hatred. It always made me feel horrible. Finally, one time I yelled at him that all he was doing was making me feel bad about myself on top of feeling bad. He got it. He never did it again.

Positive thinking can also lead to something I call the *enlightenment trap*: trying to feel and think the right thing, but it is not authentic. Some people can say positive things convincingly, but it is only skin-deep at best. Churchgoers and priests who say one thing, but are lying to themselves and everyone else, living secret lives that are exactly the opposite of what they espouse, are *not present*. They have fallen deep into the *enlightenment trap*. They talk a good game, but they are playing quite a different one.

In acting, trying to manipulate oneself into feeling a certain way leads to inauthentic acting. The moment we feel obligated to feel a certain way that feeling dries up. The same goes for life. It is why Christmas can be so difficult. We're all supposed to be so happy and joyful. No wonder it is so hard to feel happy—because we spend so much energy trying to avoid, dominate, and control the so-called darker emotions. When people call me a positive thinker now, I'm surprised. Certainly I didn't use to be one. I became one through telling myself the truth.

I do use positive reinforcement, but I think you have to be close to feeling calm to even hear anything positive. I don't attempt to use positive reinforcement in class until I'm fairly certain that the person is present. After people perform and take a great risk, they are often freaked out by their expression and by their own brilliance. They are reeling from the feelings they just went through. I must let them take conscious time to Land or they can't even hear the good things people are saying about their work. When I see the glassy look in their eyes, I will stop and help them get present so they can hear what people are saying.

If you are plunging down the road in reverse, you'll only strip your gears trying to use positive thinking. You must be present first. Then, when you get to a neutral gear, you can start to go forward. It is like the scuba diving instruction I heard before going on a dive, "The current down there is very strong today. When it goes against you, keep swimming easily—relax, and watch the reef go by the wrong way. When the current is with you, swim like hell."

THE KEY TO RELAXATION

Given how important it is to be relaxed, and given how difficult it is to be authentically relaxed, what in the world can we actually do to become relaxed? Is there a key to Relaxation? Yes. And as with Being Present, the key is simple but not easy.

The key is to *accept what you feel*. This may be all you need to master relaxation. There is tremendous transformational power in acceptance. Literally thousands of times, I have watched students Get Present and noticed that the very instant they *accept* their sensations, there is a perceptible physical Relaxation, some organic shift that can be observed. Sometimes it is just a little drop in the shoulders, but it is always visible and evident. Aiming for acceptance works even when your body is vibrating with intense feeling.

Oprah Winfrey was interviewing a famous golfer. She asked him how he could be so relaxed under so much pressure. He laughed and told her that was only how he looked on the outside. Inside, he felt intense feelings and then added that he *liked* the feelings. In other words, he accepted them, reveled in them, and didn't resist them at all. That is Relaxation. He plays golf because he loves to play golf. The man knew how to Be Present, Relax, and Commit.

However, many of us do not like intense feelings. We resist them and fear them. Unfortunately, *resistance creates persistence*. As the saying goes, *what we resist persists*. Most of us know that. We *know* that we're not supposed to resist our feelings, but they're hard not to resist. They can be scary.

Don't worry. There is a wonderful trick that will get you through any resistance: *accept resistance*. When a student says to me, "I'm resisting this feeling," I don't try to push him through it. Instead, I ask what the resistance feels like, and ask him if he can accept it. *Resistance shows up physically in many ways that are uncomfortable*: feeling dead, tense, cut off, disembodied, stuck, or numb. Resistance itself is unpleasant. However, the moment we accept our own resistance, we're moving through it. Paradoxically, *accepting resistance melts resistance*. It really is true, but it must be authentic acceptance to work. There is no faking it.

Remember: *learning how to accept where you are will be the most powerful step you can take toward Relaxation*. If you feel sad and you hate feeling sad, first accept that you hate it and that it is okay to hate it. Really let yourself hate feeling sad fully until you naturally go to the next level, which is accepting your sadness.

It is like the joke about the guy on Seventh Avenue in New York City who asks a passerby how to get to Carnegie Hall and is told, "Practice! Practice! Practice!" How you get to Relaxation is by *acceptance, acceptance, acceptance*. And truly, acceptance takes practice, practice, practice. Once you are present in your body, you will be calm enough to start retraining your mind.

NON-JUDGMENT

The more you can accept what you feel, the more you can consciously choose to practice non-judgment. An actor is never served by judging himself. In an interview in *TheaterWeek*, Judd Hirsch emphasized that when he was able to give up judgment (criticism), he was freed completely as an actor. He realized the only important thing is commitment from a place of love.

Good actors know that they cannot judge the characters they play. Judging will lead to commenting on the character—a kind of distancing that leads to bad acting. As actors, we must always find something within a character to love and that elicits our compassion. It is the challenge. To be a brilliant Willy Loman or Blanche DuBois, you have to love that character with all his or her problems and flaws. To be a brilliant you, you have to love yourself with all of your problems and flaws. Commit to not judging yourself.

SELF-FORGIVENESS

As a performer, my Relaxation is constantly tested. The opening night of *Cloud 9* I missed an entrance—a whole entrance! I didn't show up for a short scene. Admittedly, I was playing two characters, changing back and forth between them with twelve costume changes, and always entering from somewhere else on the set. It was a nightmare. Still, I missed it! Unforgivable! Opening night! How could I?

I honestly don't remember much of the rest of the night, but I vividly remember sitting on a bench backstage for the thirty seconds I had until the next entrance. I was paralyzed with horror and shock that I had missed an entrance. A voice like an angel inside me spoke. "Well," it said. "You can either let your mistake ruin the rest of the performance, or you can choose to forgive yourself right this instant. Which is it?"

I chose to forgive myself, and dashed on stage. The rest of the performance was fine. No one even mentioned my missed entrance later.

Can you forgive yourself for the mistakes you have made? Can you pick yourself up when you fail and keep going?

LETTING GO OF CONTROLLING

Practice letting go of trying to control life. Trying to control is an automatic response to fear. We will do anything to maintain control, even destroy our lives. Because performing arouses so much fear, the impulse of actors is to want to control their performances and put them in safe little boxes. I cringe when people say, "You nailed that performance!" People who try to repeat that "nailed" performance end up with dead, stock performances that are lifeless and uninspired. It is the same in life. Authentic acting and creating require *not controlling*. It is the essence of much comedy. Bette Midler, Steve Martin, and Jim Carrey drive us to out-of-control laughter because of their daring lack of controlling.

When performers have the courage to let go of trying to control and instead be fully present and express where they are, the very air is electrified and enlivened. One of my major tasks as a teacher is to help students loosen their grip, let go, and just free-fall. "Let go, let Creativity" equals "Let go, let God."

There are distinctions to be made: letting go of controlling does not mean letting go of control. The one rule in my classes is you must not hurt yourself, someone else, or break the furniture. That would be letting go of control, going on a rampage, running amok. That's not it. It is actually not a difficult distinction to get. Most students get it right away and are able to let go of controlling their feelings without going nuts.

It is the same kind of distinction between chaos and freedom. Freedom requires boundaries; otherwise, it is just chaos.

Letting go of controlling also does not mean not participating—lying there like a dead fish and letting life do you. No. We must also be committed and take steps along our path. Just as an actor must prepare—learn the lines, take all the necessary steps, and then let go—so must we do our laundry, take each step in front of us, and then let go. It is a dance. It is love-making with creativity and life.

There is a Buddhist concept called *near enemy*. I understand it to mean close but vastly different. For instance, denial can have the appearance of acceptance, but they are vastly different. So it is with submission and surrender. They are not the same thing—close in appearance, but worlds apart in experience. Surrendering is a powerful choice. It must be chosen and conscious—otherwise, it is a kind of submission. Love is the basis of surrender; force is the basis of submission. Conscious surrender is not something we Westerners understand easily.

My first day on the film *Suspect* was harrowing. I had been hired by the director sight unseen to play Congresswoman Grace Comisky. Though I am not certain how I got the job, I believe Cher's recommendation had something to do with it.

When I arrived in Washington, I was taken to her trailer to meet the director. Cher was very friendly. We chatted about old times when we had worked in the movie *Silkwood* together.

The director sat off to the side and said nothing. I felt studied and judged. He scared the hell out of me. I became certain that he decided he did not like me and was sorry he had hired me. After an uncomfortable half hour, I was taken back to my hotel.

Normally, I do not suffer from insomnia, but that night I could not sleep. The next morning I got up at five A.M., and started on a day of appointments with congresswomen and shopping for costumes.

I reported to the set at six P.M. for a night shoot at the Treasury building. There was no dressing room within walking distance. I had to sit in a large room with many extras.

All night long I was told my scene would be next—which was why I couldn't go to my dressing room.

At two-thirty A.M. we broke for lunch. I found myself at the restaurant seated next to the director who turned his body away from me and never once spoke to me during the meal.

The meal over, I was returned to the large room with uncomfortable chairs, and I continued waiting. "Your scene will be next," I was told often. It wasn't. I was beginning to feel that I was being deliberately abused. I thought I would faint from the tension.

At six A.M. the night's shoot was over. I was immensely relieved. I had been there twelve hours under physical discomfort and anxiety. I knew I could deal with it all if I could just go back to the hotel, get some sleep, and recover.

At that moment, an assistant came to me and told me to get ready. We were going overtime and my scene was next—this time for real. I was horrified. Gone was my excitement about the role and script and working with Dennis Quaid. My body was screaming with fatigue. All I wanted to do was lie down and die. I had gone two nights without sleep. I was practically hallucinating with fatigue.

The makeup man and the hairdresser called me over to a high canvas chair while they tried to fix me up. I was certain that I was not going to be able to do the scene. I couldn't even remember any of the lines. I was convinced that the director was a monster who just wanted to humiliate me and fire me in front of hundreds of people. It was the end of my career.

I closed my eyes and gave up. I could feel the makeup brushes on my face and the comb teasing my hair for my big hairstyle. I was deeply exhausted. I got present with my body and surrendered to my fatigue. It was like falling into hell. I didn't think there would be a bottom. Down, down, down through the nausea. I had the thought that when I actually hit the bottom of my exhaustion, I would die. Well, if I did, at least I wouldn't be fired. It was a way out. I kept falling. Now I could barely feel the makeup brush or the comb. I somehow managed to stay in the chair while I surrendered to the endless fall through my fatigue and tension.

I hit bottom. I didn't die. Instead, it suddenly all became hilariously funny. My career was over? So what? The worst that was going to happen was that I would go back to Connecticut and live my life. I started to laugh. The makeup man and the hairdresser didn't know what I was laughing at, but because it was so genuine or we were all fatigue-giddy, they started laughing with me. Soon, everyone in the room was laughing—a whole roomful of two hundred glum and tired extras laughing with me—even though they hadn't been told any joke. I laughed and laughed. Suddenly, I was wide-awake and relaxed.

I went out to the set. The director mapped out complicated movements for the first scene with Dennis Quaid. By the time the marks were taped on the floor, it looked like a Fred Astaire dance. I went to my entrance spot behind impressive carved bronze doors. I was a little nervous, but I was *there*. I really didn't care whether the director liked me or not. I was going to just do what I do.

My cue came. I went through the door, went to Dennis, hit my marks and Communicated. Fortunately, Dennis Quaid was very present and is a great communicator. Working with Dennis was like finding a life preserver in a stormy ocean. We did the scene in one take.

Afterward, I went to the catering table to get myself a rewarding cup of tea. The director suddenly appeared beside me, a completely different man, chatty, making jokes. I must have turned to him with such an expression of wide-mouthed disbelief that he responded, "Well," he said in a hearty British accent, "You know when you've done a good job, don't you?" (nudge-nudge, wink-wink) "It's when the director talks to you *ahfter* the shot!"

I wanted to punch him. I didn't.

What had saved me was surrendering completely to what I was feeling and what was happening. It was a lesson I never forgot about the importance of not only being present—but fully embracing and surrendering to where I was.

SPIRITUALITY AND RELAXATION

It may not be possible to be completely relaxed without having some kind of spiritual life. This does not mean you have to devote yourself to a religion or a guru. Being spiritual does not mean you must hold any particular belief. I define spiritual as anything that increases your awareness and makes you feel better about yourself, the world, and the Universe.

Therefore, a spiritual experience can range from eating a juicy, delicious tomato to having a cosmic epiphany. By this definition, great suffering, illness, and loss can be spiritual as long as you can find in them a meaning that fulfills this definition. Spirituality is a choice. It is both based on and results in trust, acceptance, truth, love, faith, and hope. The highest spiritual game we seem to be playing on this earth is *not knowing and trusting anyway.*

There is a term in acting which amounts to advice: act *as if.* Act *as if* you are a king or queen. Act *as if* you would if you were in that situation. It would be wonderful if we could all approach a role, an audition, going out on stage, or confronting any situation *as if* it is going to work out fine.

One always has a choice: to act from fear or from courage. Acting *as if* whatever we are facing is going to turn out well can help us get through it. The more we do that, the more we find out that yes, indeed, it *was* okay, and we did get through it.

Spirituality is acting as if there is order and meaning in the Universe even if we don't fully understand it. When we act as if there is no order and nothing but chaos in the Universe, it is a lot more difficult to get through a situation, let alone the rest of our lives. Take the actor's advice. *Act* as if *you believe in yourself and can do what is in your heart to do.*

Fear and excitement are experienced almost precisely in the same places in one's body. The difference is in the context. Fear is the mind saying, "This is not going to work out! Dreadful things are coming!" Fear transforms to excitement when the mind says, "Oh, wow! This is going to be great! I'm really looking forward to it! I know it is going to work out!"

RE MINDERS

Cynics question why there are so many self-help books. "If they worked," they grouse, "wouldn't *one* of them be enough?" No. Because we constantly need to be re minded. Every day. Our minds have some deep programming that goes way back into the DOS (remember DOS?—ever heard of DOS?) of our collective unconscious. It is hard to locate that programming, let alone redo it. One book, one day, or one workshop isn't going to do it. We must dedicate ourselves to transformation on a daily basis. Actors must rehearse until the lines are second nature. We have to practice new ways of thinking, being, and speaking until it becomes second nature as well.

Re minders are positive thinking, one may remind me, but to me, it is really about making the choice between trust and fear. When I am in a calm state, re minders help me to recommit to trust. I have different books I return to when I feel the urge for a little re minding: among them are *A Path With Heart* by Jack Kornfield, *Tao Te Ching* by Stephen Mitchell, and *Emmanuel* by Pat Rodegast and Judith Stanton.

It can be argued that there is nothing new under the sun—that nothing anyone says is anything other than ancient knowledge. Yet we do get new insights and new perspectives that are available if we are willing to listen to others. Someone may say something that you may have heard in other forms over and over again for many years; but because you are ready to hear it, and someone expresses it in a way that somehow reaches you, you have a "new" insight—a minor or major epiphany.

BELIEFS

Choose the beliefs that create Relaxation. Use the injunction of many twelve-step programs to *take what works, and leave the rest,* including anything in this book. Beliefs are just beliefs. And a belief is only as good as its ability to make you feel better. Beliefs are tricky because we often deceive ourselves into thinking that our beliefs are the truth. "There is a God." "There is no God." "You create it all." "You are powerless."

When we carefully examine most of what we firmly think of as the truth, we will find that an astonishing amount of it is actually belief. There may be a great number of people who agree with our belief, which gives it the imprimatur of truth, but it is still a belief. Once we understand that most of what we think is indeed based on a belief system, we are freer to choose the beliefs that will create the context for Relaxation.

In *Even Cowgirls Get the Blues*, Tom Robbins wrote, "If you don't like your life, change the way you look at it." Beliefs must serve you. If they don't, throw them out. What serves one person may or may not serve another. The belief that there is no God may comfort one person and terrify another. The belief "you create it all" made my friend Anna feel horrified and guilty when she discovered she had cancer. To her, "I am powerless" was infinitely more comforting. It allowed her to take care of herself, do what she had to do to get well, and leave the rest to God.

"What you fear you will create." That idea scared the hell out of me. It made me afraid of being afraid. Fear then looked like a dangerous but powerfully creative tool. I was sitting on a plane thinking about that—trying very hard not to be afraid of the plane crashing so as not to *create* the plane crashing. My fear was not just the elephant in the room, it was galloping up and down the aisle. I was afraid to look at or it would trample me.

Then I remembered my great grandmother, who often said, "What you worry about never happens." After my father died when I was very young, in a crazy application of that belief, I took on worry as my job. After all, I hadn't worried about him dying. Maybe if I had worried about it, he wouldn't have died. I spent much of my youth thinking up every horrible possibility I could just to make certain none of it would happen.

Neither belief "What you fear you create" nor "What you worry about never happens" ever served to increase my Relaxation.

The pilot told us to fasten our seat belts as we were heading into turbulence. It was in that moment that I got it about beliefs, all beliefs: any belief is just a belief, not the truth. I relaxed. I tossed those beliefs out the window and smiled as we bumped our way through the sky.

Hey, if what you tell me or what I tell myself doesn't help me to relax, I'm going to do what I can to let it go and aim for Relaxation, because *Relaxation is what works.* I am more interested in what works than being right. One of the greatest uses of our minds is to use them to *create the contexts for Relaxation. Instead of choosing to believe that you cannot get what you want, choose to believe that you can and you will.* It will make it so much easier to take action.

VALIDATE!

One of the most powerful tools for creating Relaxation is validation. Commit to validating yourself and everyone around you. It works. Having used validation as a teaching technique with actors for many years now, I am utterly convinced of its power to create growth and healing—especially with new ideas, embryonic creations, and seedlings.

I attended a class taught by Dan Fauci. As part of my first class, Dan focused on what worked about my performance. I had never experienced a teacher doing that. It was shocking, eye-opening, and had a profound effect on me. No criticism?! What a concept. This was how he approached every student's first class.

When I was asked to teach, I decided to do the same thing as an experiment—not only in the first class but in every class. I wanted to do for my students what Dan Fauci and many directors, like June Havoc, Mike Nichols, and Tommy Tune, had done for me. They had trusted me and respected me and believed in me more than I did in myself. I blossomed in their validation.

As a teaching tool, validation works beyond anything I ever imagined. I began to see that people have no idea what really works about them. I also noticed that as students realized they were not going to be criticized or attacked, they would relax and begin to take chances and risks in their work.

In the beginning it was difficult for me. I was used to seeing only through eyes that judged and focused on what didn't work. I had to choose to validate and trust a student's process. I had to resist my own desires to push, shove, and control. Sometimes it was a difficult search to find something that worked. It doesn't mean I have no negative judgments and criticisms. It means I don't give them any air time. I bring my attention to what does work.

Validating does not mean I relinquish coaching students. I do coach. But my coaching is not based on criticism or what seems "wrong." I coach them to fulfill The Four Principles. I am *not* talking about lying or inventing something nice to say. I am talking about focus. Validation is a choice. I can be just as "right" invalidating something as I can be validating it.

I joke that I train actors the way dolphins are trained. I once did volunteer work with dolphins and discovered, to my surprise, that often dolphins themselves come up with flips and twists, and their trainers whistle their approval. Having been validated, dolphins repeat what the audience applauds. Dolphins, like people, are encouraged through validation.

Also, I decided not to choose work for a student. I do not tell people what to do. I never assign work. I simply ask them what they want to do. I get out of the way. I become what I call No Wind.

When students come to class, they are so used to walking against the wind of criticism and being told what to do that when I don't, they sometimes fall flat on their faces and become disoriented.

"Tell me what to do!" they plead. "How will I improve if you don't criticize me?" Their muscles are used to struggle. They panic. They get angry at me. Some leave. Some get it and stay. Then. Oh, then. Once they get it, they start running. They fly. What a joy it is for me to watch that. Their uniqueness emerges.

There is a genius in people waiting for a safe space in which to be born. This genius can lurk in the very places that at first don't seem to work. When they are not criticized, these so-called faults or flaws can transform into what is fascinating and even marketable about a person.

Validation is a great key to teaching. In an experimental study, teachers were given classes of so-called exceptional students who were in fact previously considered to be average. But because the teachers were told that the students were exceptional, they created the space for the students to *be* exceptional. And they were. It is tragic that so much of our schooling is based on criticism, invalidation, and comparison.

What works in teaching works in life, as I quickly discovered. I remember hearing of a psychiatrist who was treating a woman who said she couldn't get a job. All she wanted to do was sit still for hours without moving. So, he validated that by suggesting she get a job as an artist's model. She did.

According to the dictionary, something is *valid* if it has "legal efficacy or force." *To validate* means "to make legally valid" and "to grant official sanction to by marking." *Validation* is active. Therefore, Communication is inherent in validation. The more we validate ourselves and one another, the more we can trust ourselves and one another. The more we validate, the safer we feel. The more we validate, the more we love. The more we validate, the more acceptable everything and everyone seems. The negative can be transformed into the positive by finding what is valid in it.

Validation also empowers the person who is validating. The fact is I can only see in you what is true about me. Therefore, if I validate what is true about you, I am also validating and empowering what is true about me.

The cause of validation is love. The result of validation is increased love. Validation nurtures possibility and allows for the process of growth. Greatness blooms in the space created by validation. It is to a human being as rain and sun and good soil are to a rose. It has been proven that plants grow larger and healthier when they are given loving thoughts and kind words. So it is with people.

Start to really look at what works in the people closest to you and validate it. Start looking at what really works in you and validate it. What doesn't work will simply melt away or be transformed into your genius. Do you secretly want to slit throats? Become a throat surgeon. You'll get paid a lot of money for slitting throats.

Some people and things are easier to validate than others. A rose may be easier than a cockroach, but it is quite possible to validate cockroaches. "Congratulations. You are one of the oldest, unchanging life forms on this planet. You have lasted millions of years. You are undaunted and prolific, and no matter how much we try to kill you, you adapt and adapt in order to survive. What a life force you have!" Remember! *Validation must come from truth. Don't lie. Don't make it up.* It is not positive thinking. It is seeing what is actually there.

Criticism is like taking a tender shoot and pouring acid rain on it or yanking on it to make it grow faster. The wonder is that the urge toward creativity is so strong that it springs up even in spaces not conducive to growth: saplings can break through the concrete on old highways. How much better to validate and create lush gardens! Try validation as an experiment. See what happens.

THANK YOUR BLOCKS

Amazing breakthroughs happen when we even learn to validate resistance and thank our blocks. An actress came to my workshop. Her goal was "to cry." She had not been able to cry for years. When she got present, she felt as if a steel plate were across her heart. It was bolted into place with thick, huge bolts that were vivid in her mind's eye. "Thank that plate," I said gently. "You obviously needed it. It protected you." That surprised her. The idea was new to her. She had assumed she was supposed to blowtorch her way through the steel or wrench open the bolts. They were strong, huge bolts. "Just reach out and touch them gently." As soon as she did, she burst into tears.

The blocks and defenses that we created as children actually saved our lives. We were clever to come up with them. Unfortunately, these same defenses can ruin our lives when we're adults. No longer attached to our survival, they become terribly destructive. They must be dismantled. But in order to do so, we must honor them, and thank them.

A three-year-old girl was thrown out of a car in the middle of a highway by her insane mother. It was a busy, four-lane highway. She could have died. She was found, alive but terrified, clinging to a chain-link fence that separated the lanes of the highway. As horrifying as that story is, I found myself concerned by the ending: the person who rescued her *pried* her fingers lose from the fence. I wished that the person could have helped the little girl *choose* to let go of the fence—taken the time to let her choose—helped her to honor the fence—helped her to thank it and herself for grabbing on and saving her own life. Unfortunately, she might spend the rest of her life building fences to cling to when she feels threatened.

How vital it is to learn how to honor the fences (honor defenses). Until we can experience and validate the resistance, the numbness, the cement in our veins, the woodenness, the steel plates over our hearts, we cannot let them go. Don't resist resistance. Don't indulge it through your actions, either. Experience your defenses and thank them in order to let go of them.

GIVE IT TO THE CHARACTER

One of the strangest but truest things about acting is that good actors cannot help but *become* the characters they are portraying in some way. It can be very subtle and sly and difficult to see. Sometimes it is ridiculously obvious.

My first big part in college was Raina in Shaw's *Arms and the Man*. I fell madly in love with the leading man. In the next five plays I also fell in love with all my leading men. I noticed that after the plays were over, I wasn't so much in love with them any more. Playing romantic parts can be dangerous to marriages. I'm certain it is one of the reasons Hollywood marriages fall apart so easily and quickly. You're off on some exotic location, pretending you are madly in love with someone, it easy to think it is real.

Every time someone gets up in my class to work and gets present, what they are feeling is amazingly and elegantly appropriate to the character. Very often the actors believe that what they are feeling is wrong, but it never is. A student gets up to do a scene. She starts trembling with terror. "This is all wrong," she insists. "This doesn't feel like Medea."

"Just feel what you're feeling, and start from there," I say. She stands in her terror and begins. The moment she speaks, rage and power sear the air. What she does is scary and powerful and couldn't be better or more exciting.

Afterward, we could both see how appropriate her terror was. She *was* Medea without any judgment or pretense. Her fear fueled all the hatred and rage she needed to realize the role. Medea's terrible actions are based on her fears for herself and the lives of her own children.

I am always amazed at how much people unconsciously take on the feelings of characters and think the feelings are about themselves. I try to help actors understand this. I urge them to give everything they think and feel to the character and not to take any of it on personally when they are working on a role. It is difficult not to do. It requires vigilant, conscious effort.

I know. I've done it for years. As actors, we are almost always surprised by this phenomenon. It catches us unaware. We may feel angry, or think we are failures, or fall in love, and not realize that these feelings belong to the character. Experiencing all the emotional underbelly of a character may be uncomfortable, but our discomfort is actually *information* about the character that we need to know. Through our own emotional responses, we can plumb the roles we are playing and bring depth to them in performance.

What does "Give it to your character" have to do with life? Well, just about everything.

GIVE IT TO YOUR INNER CHILD

As acting students learn to give everything they think and feel to the character, we must learn to give our difficult, reappearing feelings and thoughts to our own inner child.

A friend once said, "I project onto anything that moves." I found that extremely funny because it is so true. It is our inner child who projects onto anything and everything that moves. Oh we think our intense emotions are about the present-day situation, but invariably the feelings point back to our childhood. As a guideline, the more upset we are, the more our inner children are being triggered.

And just like actors who have such a difficult time understanding that what they feel belongs to their characters, so do we find it hard to realize that our most uncomfortable feelings belong to our inner children. So often we do not actually see the present—especially when we are upset—because we are dragging our past into the present. We see through the eyes of the hurt or wounded child within. Emotions blur our vision. So it is vital that we learn not to make judgments or draw conclusions about our lives in the middle of emotional upset. Unfortunately, *that* is exactly the time we do make all kinds of ill-considered decisions and draw incorrect conclusions.

Projection is not a bad thing. As in acting, it can be a tool. It offers us information we have not known before. It helps us to understand and move forward. This phenomenon happens in my classes a lot—which is why an acting class veers so close to therapy—especially because our creative source *is* our inner child.

I do my best to keep the focus on my purpose: to help people *create* and to get the creations out into the world. But sometimes, in order to do that, the creative inner child must come forward, be seen, and express without doing damage. This can be messy. But if students understand that they are projecting old, unexpressed stuff onto the role or other cast members, the air clears up. Although my classes aren't therapy, as a by-product, I have seen students transform and grow and heal and change in remarkable ways as they develop more awareness of and compassion toward their inner children.

Intense feelings that were too difficult to face in the original situation can be experienced now with adult consciousness. When we feel what our inner children could not, we go on what I call *rescue missions*—recovering the creativity and life force that got lost, stymied, strangled, stuffed, or suppressed. It takes courage.

In Greek mythology Demeter never gives up trying to rescue her daughter, Persephone, from Hades. And she must do it every spring—just as we must go on many missions to rescue our inner children and bring them back to life.

We're like trees. Every year we have lived is inside us like the rings in a tree. It is there to be tapped, and we can re-experience every age we have ever been. And, because we are conscious beings, we can go back inside and heal.

So when we project onto others, it is important to remember this is an opportunity for a much deeper self-knowledge and self-empowerment. It helps us to get in touch with what we need to know about ourselves and to look at what was rejected in us that needs to be loved, embraced, and integrated.

When we go back and rescue feelings and parts of ourselves that need attention and healing, we will then have more energy and be clearer about our path and the options before us. Whereas conscious projection as an information guide and healing tool can be a good thing, unconscious projection ruins jobs and relationships. It is a destructive force. When we are in the throes of unconscious projection, we are not present.

Knowing that you're projecting does not mean that you will not feel all the feelings. On the contrary, it should give you the self-compassion to feel the feelings as fully and as long as they last, so that you can rescue and love that neglected, unknown, dear, truthful, creative, wise child inside you. The inner child does not need to be squelched or indulged but championed. What does your inner child really need and want? How can you supply those things for yourself in a healthy empowering way?

Always be willing to listen to your inner child—let your inner child feel—but don't let your inner child draw conclusions and make life decisions from the feelings. The thinking will be a child's thinking. We need to find the balance and integration in order to live full, complete, and loving lives. Like the old saw "all work and no play," all adult and no inner child, or all child and no responsible adult leads to terrible imbalances.

How does one distinguish between intuition and the unfelt feelings of your inner child? Unfelt feelings will probably be urging you to take action immediately. Quit your job! Get out of the relationship! Hide! Go away! The voice will be loud and urge immediate action to either do or not something. Your mind may come up with many rational reasons why you must act or do something right now, but be suspicious of yourself. If you can, unless the situation is actually urgent (the room is on fire), sit with the feelings and ask yourself how they relate to your inner child. If there is no immediate cause for action, take time to Be Present. Let feelings be felt fully. Don't do anything. Just feel. When you are calmer, you will see options that you didn't see before.

Intuition, on the other hand, is subtler. It has a quieter voice. One needs to be calm to hear it. Intuition can rarely speak in the middle of loud emotion. Your mind may not even want to hear what your intuition is telling you. Listen to that quiet voice. Try not to give the really loud voices in your head much credence.

PLAY

Play. As we get older, we tend to lose touch with playing— purposeless, just-having-fun kind of play. But *playing creates Relaxation*. It is hard to be tense when you're having fun and laughing a lot—maybe impossible. So many people have written about the curative power of laughter and play. One of the traps of being a professional actor is how easy it is to lose a sense of play. Everything becomes so important and serious. I remind my students that their sense of love of acting, their joy in doing it is precious. If they lose that, they lose everything. Their acting will be dead. It will be lacking something that is not easily defined but very apparent. "Remember! You're doing something called a *play*. Try not to forget it." *Creativity is play.*

If we could hold the context that everything is play, we could take a giant step toward Relaxation. "All the world's a stage, and we are merely players." Someone is called *a player* who can work the game of life to his or her own advantage.

I read about a C.E.O. who thinks his job is the most terrific fun he can imagine. To him, it is play. To be able to take life not so seriously is high mastery. When things become too significant and important, we become attached to them. That is certainly the tendency in an acting career. Once that happens, an actor's work suffers as a result. I have known actors just starting out who arrive in New York and get cast at their first audition. They are not yet taking it all too seriously. They breeze into an audition, and their innocence is mistaken for confidence.

People are often shocked when they discover how much doctors and nurses joke during surgery. The joking is not an indication that they do not take their jobs seriously or that they are shut down to the importance and responsibility. On the contrary,

91

the joking relieves the tension and helps them to relax enough to do their best work.

When I played Sabina in *The Skin of Our Teeth* in Seattle, I found myself hanging out with the non-professionals in the cast. They were full of playfulness and inventiveness. They horsed around in rehearsals and created a camaraderie and liveliness that was missing in the professionals who, by contrast, were embittered, dull, and very serious about their work. In spite of the difficulties with the production (in the first preview the set changes between acts took longer than the acts themselves) I had a lot of fun because I had immersed myself in the spirit of play with the non-professionals.

It is difficult to remember *it is just a play*.

A play that I had written and worked on many years, called *Juno's Swans*, finally got a production at the Second Stage Theatre in New York City. With a good cast and director it was doing very well in previews. Audiences laughed and loved it. Performances were selling out. Producers brought backers and telephoned me, anxious to produce the play.

Opening night it all fell apart. Though there were many good reviews, the *New York Times* critic yawned at it. Unfortunately, the *Times* review is the only one that counts to the producers of plays in New York. Thus *Juno's Swans* was doomed to oblivion. The producers and backers disappeared into the woodwork. My world crashed in a minute. The opening-night party broke up early and sadly.

At home that night I lay in bed feeling as if my body had been shot through with a howitzer—nothing but a gaping hole where my heart used to be. The feeling was so dramatic that all I could do was lie there and feel it. I thought I was going to die.

The next day a friend invited me over to her pool. It was a gorgeous June day. A perfect day. I lay on the lounge chair looking at the perfect sky, feeling the warmth of the sun. She put a piña colada in my hand. I sipped the delicious, icy drink. "So," I said. "This is what failure feels like." I nibbled a chip and sipped some more of my piña colada and laughed. "Hmmm. This is not so bad. I can live through this." And, of course, I did.

Importance, significance, and fear are all wet blankets to creativity and play. Unfortunately, the least fun I have had in the theater was in the Broadway shows I did in which there was a constant background hum of fear that manifested in tension, distrust, competition, and lowered creativity. Playing is not merely a good idea; it must be encouraged and cultivated.

So many times during the Olympics I've heard gold medalists say, "I just wanted to have fun." And they *won*.

The trick is to really *care* about something or someone and still hold it lightly—to be fully Committed *and* Relaxed at the same time. The two principles are not in conflict. Relaxation actually *serves* the Commitment. If you've lost your sense of play, do what you can now to recover it.

THE ULTIMATE KEY TO RELAXATION

If acceptance is the basic key to acquiring Relaxation, trust is the ultimate one. To be completely relaxed in life, choose to trust life. Trust is the province of the innocent/fearless and the wise/brave. It takes a great act of courage to trust—like the cinematic moment when Indiana Jones stepped from a cliff onto a path that looked invisible. He willed himself to walk out into space in a conscious act of trust and found himself on solid ground. Every day we live is a little like that moment. Trust is a belief that things are going to work out even when we don't know how.

A student performs a scene in class. He's very present. He's definitely committed. He's communicating, but even though he is playing a king and yelling and stomping around the stage, he doesn't seem powerful. The woman playing opposite him, standing more quietly center stage, seems to have all the power in the scene no matter how much he rages. The man is a very good actor, so the scene works in a way. His lack of power is even funny, but the balance of power is off. What's missing? *Relaxation.*

I talk with him and ask him to *believe that he is going to get what he wants no matter what she says.* The next week he does the scene with this adjustment, and the balance of power is more on his side. *Actors often mistakenly think expressed rage is power. It is not. It is the expression of impotence.*

Trust and Faith are the highest forms of Relaxation you can achieve. When you can, as often as you can, choose the context of trust. When you can't, just feel your feelings without attaching them to a condemnation of God, yourself, or the Universe. I don't know anyone who isn't at least a little nervous about the idea of death or dying. I don't know anyone who hasn't experienced losses—sometimes great ones. I don't know anyone who hasn't suffered the slings and arrows of outrageous fortune—who hasn't been banged around and bumped by life, who hasn't had accidents and found themselves in dead-ends or on paths that seem to go nowhere, who hasn't faced situations that seem frightening. All of these experiences can be presented before the jury to prove that life sucks and there is no meaning to it—all sound and fury signifying nothing. One can make an excellent case for that.

However, and it is a big however, the people who choose—and it is a choice—to trust that there is some kind of divine order to the Universe—who choose that somehow things are going to work out for the best no matter how it may look in the present—who choose that there is some good to be gleaned from an unpleasant situation or illness, *they* are the people whose lives work better for having made that choice. Therefore, to choose to trust life is what works—if you are interested in living a more peaceful, happy, healthy, and successful life. It is a choice that has to be made over and over again.

You get fired from a job. What do you do? Panic? Decide that you're not going to make it? Or, feel your fear and choose that it was a good thing you got fired because a better situation is up the road? Could you feel your fear knowing that the job wasn't really the best one for you even though you probably never would have quit had it been up to you?

Suppose the one to whom you have devoted your life suddenly announces she wants a divorce. It is not what you want. It is an unexpected slap in the face. It bruises your ego. What do you do? Become enraged and tell her she has ruined your life? Try to ruin hers? Or, feel your hurt, and face the fact that the marriage was not all it could have been anyway? Could you feel your fear of the future and hold the thought that there is another woman who will show up who is much better for you and a relationship that will work beautifully? It is probably going to show up with or without your trust. Had you trusted, you might not have wasted so much time making yourself and everyone else around you miserable.

Suppose it hasn't turned out beautifully—yet—in the time you want it to? Is that still a cause for distrust? Trust and faith is holding onto the fact that it really isn't all over until the fat lady sings—no matter how it looks. Does trusting mean not taking action? No. If the situation really isn't working, it probably means there's another direction that you're supposed to go—but you are afraid to go. If there is absolutely nothing you can do, then let go and trust. This is hard to do in the crunch, but it is possible.

Dedicate yourself to authentic Relaxation. When you do, you will find yourself stepping into streams of workability and flow in which synchronistic events will seem commonplace. You will amass evidence that you can use to defend the case for trust.

One of the great re minders I have used is: *I accept where I am, and I trust the future.* Because I spent many years resisting where I was and fearing the future, this is a great re minder for me. Say it about a hundred times a day for the next year or so as if you really believe it and watch how your life transforms. Say it until you know you believe it. Of course, you only need to say it once if you really do believe it. *I accept where I am, and I trust the future.*

DEVELOP YOUR MASTER MIND

The automatic mind is interested mainly in survival. The automatic mind is based in fear. It will tell you to avoid or eliminate anything that threatens or appears to threaten survival. The automatic mind reacts to a creative risk as if it is as dangerous as a real physical threat. The heart pounds hard in both cases.

However, the master mind is invested in fulfilling your heart's desires. This means taking risks. One time I congratulated a producer on his risky production. He shrugged, "If you're not dangerous, you're dead." Great acting has that aspect of being dangerous and exciting. We like and need a bit of danger in our lives. We need and like challenges.

The master mind is not trying to kill us (though the automatic mind may think so). The master mind wants something that the automatic mind has difficulty understanding because it is so mired in fear. The master mind is about overcoming fear—surpassing it—doing what the heart and soul want in spite of fear.

CHALLENGES AND PROBLEMS

Sometimes I have begun working on a role and found it very challenging—too much, I sometimes think in the beginning. But then I end up loving that very difficult role. I know that without challenges I get bored. So, a certain level of stress is needed for aliveness in life. Our intention should not be to create nothing but ease in life, but to increase our ability to meet our challenges with ease.

Every act of creativity is about solving problems. Problems are opportunities. The angels put problems in our lives to point the way toward something that will greatly *enhance* our lives. As a result, our lives will be better than they were before the problem appeared.

So often when problems loom, we question God and the whole Universe. Why?! Why do I have to go through this?!

"Why?!" in this case, means "I don't like this one bit!" The problem, when it first shows itself, does not come equipped with an immediate solution. So, we jump to the conclusion that because we don't know the solution, there isn't one.

However, once we get through the emotional response to a problem, and we are in a calmer place and open to a solution, one will appear. The more we accept the problem, the more willing we are to get the lessons and guidance inherent in the problem, and the quicker the solution will appear. But desperately grabbing for the solution won't create one. A level of acceptance is vital before moving into the solution. That is the difficult part. That is why we must take all the time we need for our feelings, for our resistance, sadness, anger at having the problem. You will know when you are ready to accept the problem. You will know the difference between resignation and acceptance. Be patient with yourself. You'll get there. Just a smidgen of acceptance will start to turn the tide. Now, *allow* a solution to appear that will be an enhancement.

George Bernard Shaw talked about "lucky accidents" in writing. I've accidentally stumbled on solutions, or even made mistakes that when corrected were enhancements. Learning to approach challenges, problems, and even mistakes and failures as opportunities will certainly qualify you for your Relaxation mastery degree. Be where you are, and trust you will achieve your heart's desires. Commit to Relaxation now as if your life depends on it.

SUMMARY

Relaxation comes from thought. Movement toward realizing your dreams is not possible without relaxation. Use your mind to create the context for Relaxation: non-judgment, self-forgiveness, and validation.

The two basic keys to Relaxation are:

1. *Accept where you are.*
2. *Trust the future.*

COMMITMENT

Ninety-nine percent of all scenes in the theater are about love or its opposite, which is still about love.
—Michael Shurtleff, author of *Audition*, during one of his classes

Arguably, Commitment *is* the first principle. What we are committed to is the basis of all our actions. Our Commitments are what direct our paths in life. So, here we are at the first principle: Commitment. The deepest and most lasting Commitments are based in love. Great acting is based in love. As it is on stage, so it is in life.

Anwar Sadat wrote in *In Search of Identity*, "It was in Cell 54 that I discovered love is truly the key to everything...that love was a law in life. In love, life—nay, being itself—becomes possible...my point of departure became love of home (Egypt), love of all being, love of God."

Yes, fear and hatred can be the source of a kind of Commitment, but fear and hatred finally do burn themselves out. Love endures.

We are always committed to something—whether we are conscious of it or not. The point is to be aware of what we are already committed to. Of course, this requires Being Present. To what are you committed? Have you made a conscious choice? Is it based in love or fear? Does it feel authentic to you?

"Follow your bliss, and follow the path with love," say the sages. God put love in our hearts to pull us in the direction we are supposed to go. Your heart's desire is right for you. I have never known anyone whose heart's desire was wrong.

When students improvise in class, it is clear that the one with the strongest Commitment wins. When people act in scenes, they come to life when the actor commits to what that character wants—whether the character is aware of what he or she wants or not. The clearer an actor is about his or her character's Commitment, the more powerful the scene. An actor's Commitment is apparent. When Burt Lancaster wants something, you *know* it. He goes after it no holds barred. Russell Crowe's John Nash commits to his sanity in *A Brilliant Mind*. Sigourney Weaver's Ellen Ripley commits to saving Newt in *Aliens*. Ben Kingsley's Mahatma Gandhi commits to his stand in *Gandhi*. At the moment of Commitment, the music swells and the character becomes heroic.

So, what is Commitment? It is what you *love*. It is what you *believe* in. It is what you *want*. It is what you *need*. It is what you are *drawn to do*. It is what your *heart desires*. It is what *turns you on*. A great Commitment is all of these. It resonates in every place in your body: your head, your throat, your heart, your gut, and your groin. And like the heroes in all the stories, you must choose to follow your Commitment. You must take the first step.

My definition of Commitment is *to tell the truth about what you love and follow it up with action*.

Commitment is your true path—whether you like it or not. Very likely you do resist your path. Why? Because just like all the heroes in the movies, following your Commitment takes *great courage*. When you follow your deeply personal Commitments, you will start to notice how you contribute to everyone around you— even to the ones who might fear for you or want to stop you. Like Being Present, if you really want to make a contribution to the world, you will follow your heart's desires.

WHAT COMMITMENT IS NOT

The word *Commitment* has become a buzz-word. We may think of Commitment as what we *should* do. "I'm committed to losing twenty pounds." "I'm committed to quitting smoking." We tend to think of commitments as things that are hard, require effort, and cause struggle and suffering. True commitments are not New Year's resolutions. They are not impositions, duties, or obligations. They are not what other people want for you, or what you think you *should* want. They do not come from the ego. They are not goals, though there are goals in a Commitment.

Commitment is not willfulness—wanting it to come out the way you want it to come out. You can *do* it your way, like the song says, but you can't always *have* it your way. An authentic Commitment cannot involve dominating or manipulating another person—even yourself. You can be committed to having an intimate relationship, but if you're trying to get one with a person who does not want one with you, that is willfulness. You can want to climb Mount Everest, but if you insist on doing it when the weather is bad, that is willfulness. Distinguishing the difference between determination and willfulness can be subtle. A sign: willful people are not relaxed. Relaxation and flexibility are required in a true Commitment.

We also tend to think of Commitment in terms of doingness. But that is trying to take the cart somewhere before you even get the horse hooked up to it. If you are clear about your Commitment and accept it, the course of action will follow naturally. You get the horse, you get the cart, you hook them up, you climb in, you take the reins, and you go. It will be natural and without struggle. The horse is your desire to do something. If you don't have one, you can shake the reins all your want, but you won't be going anywhere.

In America we've been taught to believe that the only way to get where you want to go is through suffering and a kind of exhausting, relentless drive. Go. Go. Go. Even if we do have a horse, we mistreat it, and beat the poor thing to death. Conscious effort, probably a great deal of effort, is necessary, but struggle isn't. In fact, if struggle is predominant, it is very likely the goals will never be reached.

Commitments are not wishes or the need to be grandiose. I hear students say they want to win the lotto, get an Academy

Award, write the great novel, or be on magazine covers. These are not authentic Commitments. This is an attempt to bolster low self-esteem. True Commitments come *from* love, not in order to *get* love. This is a very dangerous area for performers and artists. Often they have emotional and psychological wounds that they think will be healed or salved if they become admirable and adored and honored.

True artists are happiest when they are sharing their gifts. It has so much more to do with expressing oneself fully than with the award that sits on the shelf or hangs on the wall. If you want those things in order to love yourself and be loved by others, it won't work. Awards don't do it. They really don't. Ellie Devers, a student, put it succinctly, "When I express myself fully, I love myself, everyone, and the world. When I don't express myself fully, I hate myself, everyone, and the world."

Commitment is not *should* or *ought* or *must*. Yes, we sometimes do what we think we should or ought or must do, but such things do not come from a heartfelt Commitment. They are obligations. Often they are in opposition to your real Commitments—against your true self.

As defined here, Commitment is *always* connected to the heart.

THE THREE POSITIONS OF COMMITMENT

Commitment has three positions. They are:

1. NO: knowing what you don't love, want, need, believe.

2. I DON'T KNOW: being open.

3. YES: knowing what you do love, want, need, believe.

The three positions can be likened to the rock-paper-scissors game in which two players simultaneously make representational hand gestures. Scissors are the first two fingers spread open, rock is a fist, and paper is the hand held flat. The point of the game is each position is both powerful and vulnerable depending on what it confronts: scissors can cut paper, but is broken by rock; rock can break scissors, but is wrapped by paper; and paper can wrap rock, but is cut by scissors. Power and vulnerability all depend on the position. Each one has its own quality of power. No one totally dominates the others. So it is with the three positions of Commitment.

Simple, yes? Yes. But not so easy. The most difficult aspect of Commitment is *telling the truth about it and taking the next step*.

Trying to change the truth or lying about the truth is what creates struggling and suffering:

"I don't want it." ("But I *should* want it.")

"I want it." ("But I *shouldn't* want it.")

"I don't know." ("But I *should* know.")

It is difficult to say which position in Commitment is actually more powerful. Depending upon the circumstances, sometimes NO is the most powerful position, sometimes YES is, and sometimes I DON'T KNOW is. People shape their lives and actors shape their careers out of these three positions. A character is defined by these three positions.

Each position demands its own kind of courage. There may be one that we *like* more than the others, but each creates our lives.

KNOWING WHAT YOU DON'T LOVE/WANT/NEED/BELIEVE IN

Every no leads to a better yes.
—John Ford Noonan, author of
A Couple of White Chicks Sitting Around Talking

This is the scissors position. It is not a negative position. It is a creative position. By cutting out what you don't want, it is easier to define what you *do* want, in life or art. Michelangelo said he created *David* by chipping away at everything that was *not David*. You cannot say YES to anything until you are able to say an authentic NO. It is a warrior's task. And NO is the Warrior Position.

Sometimes NO is the most important quality in a character or a person. Think of Gandhi saying NO to violence, or Peter Finch's Howard Beale screaming, "I'm mad as hell, and I'm not going to take it any more!" in the movie *Network*.

Saying NO can be extremely difficult, especially if you are being pressured strongly to say YES. The road to your true Commitment, if you are not already on it, may have to begin with the bravery of NO. As MSNBC television host Chris Hayes said, "Whether it is Rosa Parks on a bus, or a striking worker on a picket line, the moments that have given birth to the greatest progress are when people found the inner courage and peace to look power in the eye and say, 'No'."

I once heard of an acting teacher who based her entire teaching technique on chipping away at what was inauthentic in the actor. In our development as actors, our first and primary task may be to remove the covers imposed on our behavior—to uncover what we really feel and think—to find our point of view—and to release our intuition. This can take a lifetime.

A young man came for an interview to join my class. At first I was certain that I would not accept him. He was obese, had a slight lisp, and had absolutely *no* experience. He was a graduate of Harvard Law School and was making scads of money in a large law firm, but he hated being a lawyer and wanted to be an actor. I was appalled. Knowing how tough show biz is, I wanted to discourage him. Because other people's lives are not my business, I kept my mouth shut—fortunately. I didn't want to enroll him in my class of professional actors, but he hung in there. He kept talking. He was intelligent, funny, and I began to get a sense of his Commitment. He knew how hard show biz is. He was realistic, but determined. In spite of my concern for him, I took him into the class.

When he did his first monologue, I was worried. He had a long way to go. He wasn't present; he wasn't communicating; and he was rigid with tension. What was remarkable about him though was how intently he listened, watched, and participated in class. His improvement was astounding and a delight. He started communicating, being present, and relaxing. His own intelligence and sense of humor and energy began to emerge and shape his work.

Today he's living in Los Angeles, loving it, and earning his living as an actor having shed much of that excess weight. He's clearly on the path of love and not on the path of *should*. His Commitment to acting began with saying NO to his career in law. That took guts.

NO defines the space. NO is like the frame around a stage called the proscenium arch. NO is the boundary that creates true freedom. Without NO, there is chaos. Without NO, YES is not possible. Within the limits of NO, there is incredible joy and freedom. The clearer the NO, the freer we can feel. Parents who are afraid to say NO to their children create very unhappy people. I have a friend who has a word even better than NO. It is Mot (pronounced like "not"). Mot means absolutely NO.

Non-negotiable. No argument. No nonsense. Nothing further to talk about. Not said in a mean way. Just Mot.

Obviously, nothing but NO implodes space. Children in their Terrible Twos say NO to everything—even to things they want, such as popsicles. It is important to learn to say NO because you clearly don't want something, not because of fear, or you're just being stubborn like a two-year old.

However, when you have the courage to say NO to what you do not love or want, and follow through with your NO, then you are sculpting your life, your career, and your relationships. It sometimes takes enormous courage or perhaps a little insanity.

Kathy is a dolphin trainer. The level of her Commitment is quite impressive. She has been working at the Dolphin Research Center for more than twenty years, earning modest wages, and working long hours. The dolphins are her whole life, and she is completely happy. She loves her work and sees herself there for the rest of her days.

When she was a little girl, she dreamed of being with dolphins. Dutifully, however, she went to college fulfilling what she was supposed to do. She worked many years as a well-paid television reporter.

One day she found the courage to follow her true path, quit her job to go work with dolphins, and even faced her father's disapproval. When she told him, he said with great disdain, "Dolphins! I thought you outgrew that crap years ago."

She bravely said NO to what she didn't want and created the space to say YES to what she did want. Is she insane? Yes. She's insanely *happy*.

People want to wait to say NO to something until they have something to replace it. However, the way it works is that sometimes we must say NO to something *first* in order to create the space for something that we *do* want.

In *Dance While You Can*, Shirley MacLaine tells a story about Mike Nichols. One night they were to shoot a sequence in *Postcards from the Edge*, and Mike decided that the walls were the wrong color. He didn't want that color. So he had them change the color. It took three to four hours. On a movie shoot three to four hours is an incredibly expensive wait. Yet he had the guts to say NO he didn't want that color; he wanted another one.

Saying NO to what you don't want does not mean you are unloving, mean, or dominating—just clear. Mike also gives other people the space to have what they want. He's probably the only director I can ever remember saying to me during the making of *Silkwood*, "How do you want to do this scene?" I was so astounded and pleased at the question that I quickly made it up on the spot. "Well, I thought I'd start in the toilet stall, and then go to the sink to wash my face, and then go off to work." And that's how we did it—in one take.

It is disastrous to say YES when one means NO—as I well know. A few years ago I accepted an acting job against my true desires. Initially, I knew I didn't want to do it. There wasn't anything about it that enticed me. I did not believe in the material. I didn't want to commute every day. The salary was so meager that I knew it would cost me money to do the job. I didn't want to do it. I was clear. I said NO. Several times. I didn't want to do it.

Then one night I was out with several friends including the director of the piece I didn't want to do. My friends *all* thought it was a great project and urged me to take it. The director begged me to do it, jokingly threatening to kill himself if I didn't. The producer pleaded. I was flattered. I was hooked. I said YES. Then I began talking myself into it. I had many good reasons to do it. It was a review with sketches written by every famous playwright in New York: I would be seen by and work with them all. It was in New York City. So, I had every good reason to do it—*except* I was totally uncommitted to the material. So I said YES when the truth was NO.

During the rehearsal period, I experienced acute fatigue, drudgery, exhaustion, upset, and dread. I was fighting myself on every front. I tried to handle myself with a now-you've-made-your-bed-lie-in-it attitude which made it even worse. I should have let someone do the job who really *wanted* to do it!

I was in hell. I managed to get through it all, but it was unnecessarily difficult. As a learning experience, it was valuable and one I hope never to have to repeat. In fact, I stood on the street at one point and shook my fist to the sky a la Scarlett O'Hara shouting, "As God is my witness, I will never do this to myself again."

But out of that experience, I realized I had believed that if people say they love me, really love me, I have no right to tell them NO. I must do what *they* want me to do. It is not an uncommon context built out of parental training, but one that leads innocent believers to drink Kool-Aid laced with strychnine when their so-called spiritual leader tells them to.

I have learned that no matter how furious or upset people may be with me when I follow my truth and say NO to them, ultimately it is for the higher good of all.

What are the things you need to say NO to? An addiction? A bad relationship? A difficult job? Shape a new life for yourself by starting with an authentic NO. Take your power back with NO. Take care of yourself with NO.

AHDOWANNAH!

It is very important to learn the difference between "I don't want to" and *Ahdowannah!*

The best time to say "I don't want to" is right at the beginning. "Would you like to do *Medea* in Juneau, Alaska?"

"No, thanks."

That's clear.

Ahdowannah! is probably the first reaction after saying YES in the beginning. "Would you like to play *Medea* in Juneau, Alaska?"

"Oh, God. Yes! How exciting! Fabulous! I've always wanted to do *Medea. And* to go to Alaska! Far out! Yes! Absolutely!"

Now it is time to pack, sublet your apartment, find someone to feed the cat, and get on an airplane. "Ahdowannah!" cries the tired or frightened child within. You're angry at yourself for accepting the job and even think about quitting.

I read that Paul Newman called the director of *Blaze* at the last minute, saying "Ahdowannah!" It was just before shooting began. The production came to a halt. Fortunately, Newman came to his own rescue, recanting three days later.

Schedule it, and show up is an important dictum that recognizes there is probably an automatic *Ahdowannah!* response that happens at the point of Commitment. Sometimes *Ahdowannah!* can come up even before you have a chance to say YES.

Ahdowannah! is very, very sneaky. Facing something uncomfortable or frightening often brings up *Ahdowannah!* I have seen many students crash on the rock of *Ahdowannah!* They hit *Ahdowannah!* and stop coming to class. Perversely, this often happens just after they have had a major breakthrough in their acting. *Ahdowannah!* shows up most vividly during the process of Breakthrough.

Many times an actor will get up to work with a statement like, "Ahdowannah do this 'cause I'm not ready," or "Ahdowannah do what I was going to do."

"Great place to start," I respond with disgusting cheerfulness.

It actually *is* a good place to start. It is a non-controlling place to be. "Curtain going up," I say. "You're getting paid ten thousand dollars a week here. Let's go."

The student will drag herself up and stand there sullenly. "So do it wrong," I'll prod. "Throw out how you think it should be done and to hell with it. Just do it." It goes without saying that the student will often have a breakthrough.

Mastery is knowing when saying NO is valid and when it isn't. A good question to ask is, "If I could get through all the stuff *easily*, is it something I want?" If the answer is "yes," then you're up against *Ahdowannah!*

It is tricky knowing the difference between "I don't want to do this" and *Ahdowannah!*

What do you do when you schedule, show up, and then discover you don't like it? First of all, you have the choice to quit. How do you choose whether to quit or to stay? If you find out that what you're doing is immoral or evil, or you *know* you didn't really want to do it in the first place, leave. However, if you decide to stay, don't stifle your feelings. Don't stiff-upper-lip it. Be honest. It is vitally important. Don't brutalize yourself with a you-made-your-bed-now-lie-in-it attitude. Just be truthful. Do what you have to do and feel what you feel.

One time I was doing a show I loved. We got great reviews and settled into a long run. After about six months, I wanted to quit. It was a real struggle. Finally, I was able to admit to myself that I was bored. As soon as I accepted that, I was fine. I was able to put my interest back in the show.

At some point in any relationship or long run we may hit boredom. "I loved this play two years ago. Now I can't wait to get away from it." Then somehow, on the last performance love resurfaces. In life, the last days before death can also be a time to recover lost love.

Love probably doesn't ever really die; it just gets buried beneath unexpressed feelings. Sometimes they become too painful, and people have to walk away. People get worn out—with shows, with acting, and with relationships. Actors hit burnout at some time in their careers.

I had hit such a place just before I did Dan Fauci's *Mastery of Acting* workshop. I had no idea I was in such pain about acting, the business, and my career. During the workshop, I got in touch with it and expressed it so that I was able to get back in touch with my joy of acting. Soon afterward I was cast in *Cloud 9*.

"I used to love it now I don't" requires intense soul searching. It is very difficult to know whether the love is merely buried or gone. Whatever the case, trying to force yourself to continue is disastrous. Whether love is buried or momentarily lost, you need to stop to assess. It takes enormous courage to stop, especially if you or others around you are clamoring at you to continue.

LETTING GO OF WHAT DOESN'T WORK

I've noticed that one of the hardest things for most people to do is let go of what doesn't work—especially if it once worked. Sometimes things can be fixed and healed. And sometimes it becomes very clear that they can't. Yet people cannot seem to let go.

How many clothes are hanging in your closet that don't fit any more and probably never will? We hang onto things, jobs, and relationships that obviously don't work. We think we have good reasons for clinging to them. One of them is financial. Too many people find themselves in Velvet Jails (well-paying jobs or marriages to men or women with money). The price for that is terribly costly in terms of happiness and creativity. Velvet Jails may be just as hard to break out of as the ones with bars. It is a case of looks good/feels bad.

An actress took my workshop and admitted that she wanted to get rid of a bureau that she'd had for years but hated. Her inability to let it go was a symbol of the way she lived her whole life. She had a terror of letting go emotionally. Her fear was obvious during the weekend. Several months after the workshop, she wrote me a postcard with an excited message saying that she had gotten rid of the bureau. That may not seem like a big deal to you, but to her it was an enormous step toward her self-empowerment. It is very difficult to learn to let go.

So much drama is based on the unwillingness to let go. A perfect example is Miss Haversham in *Great Expectations* sitting in her wedding dress, covered in cobwebs because she can't let go of the groom who will never come.

Start practicing letting go. How about getting rid of one thing you don't want today?

SAY NO FIRMLY AND GENTLY

Emotion has energy. It attracts. Saying NO vehemently can actually attract the opposite. Strangely, the energy of fear and rage can actually draw something toward you that you don't want. I was once in a relationship where the other person compulsively tried to pick fights with me. I'm not a fighter, but I found myself getting drawn into arguments against my will. I would get frightened and start to defend myself and then get angry. I kept saying "No! I don't want to fight! Stop! Stop!" But there was fear and anger in my response. My heart would pound. I'd almost panic when I knew a fight was coming.

During this time, I was also saying NO vehemently in many areas in my life. I kept saying NO louder, and the same situations would keep coming back. My NO was not being heard and respected. One day I bottomed out with frustration and rage at my NO not being heard. I got present and realized that it was my very rage and hatred that was drawing these situations toward me. In a moment of startling clarity my Inner Wise Self said that as long as I was using so much energy on NO, there wasn't much left to pursue my YES. I needed to be both *firmer* and *gentler*.

The next time this person approached me with the tone that clearly signaled the beginning of another argument, I said very quietly but firmly, "No. You have to stop. I am not doing this ever again." And it stopped. If you find yourself saying NO to the same thing over and over again, do what you can to remove the emotional energy that you are putting into it. Be clear, firm, and calm.

Some people have a great fear of saying NO. Here are a few useful phrases for those of you who have a difficult time saying NO. There is a wonderful little book called *Getting in Touch with Your Inner Bitch* by Elizabeth Hills. Her mantra when someone asks her to do something she doesn't want to do is, "Mmmmm. I don't think so." Another useful phrase that has no blame attached to it is, "That doesn't work for me." Of course, there is always the very simple, "No, thank you."

FEAR NO/INTUITIVE NO

We sometimes say NO to something and fool ourselves into believing that our NO is authentic. When I was asked to do a play called *The Search for Signs of Intelligent Life in the Universe*, I immediately said, "Oh, no, I can't." I had at least ten good reasons—inarguable reasons.

I hung up the phone certain that I had done the right thing. Then I remembered a Commitment that I had written down about wanting to do great parts for women. The role I had just turned down is one of the all time great tour-de-force roles for women. I became a little bit suspicious of my NO.

I asked a friend to help me get present. Almost the moment she asked me what was going on in my body I was overwhelmed with terror. I shook and cried.

When I was calmer, I called the producer and accepted the job. All of my made-up reasons and considerations were not the problem. My unexperienced fear was. The role was completely in alignment with my Commitment.

I got through the job fine.

The NO that is based in fear is usually quick and loud. The intuitive NO is quieter. It speaks softly. "No thanks. I don't want that."

TELLING THE TRUTH ABOUT YOUR NO

Basically, it comes to one simple question: What is it you need to say NO to in your life?

Make a list of all the jobs, relationships, things, attitudes, and activities that you need and want to say NO to. I can already hear the *but* in your mind. "But, but, but! I should! I can't! I'd die! I'll be killed! They'll hate me."

I know. Those considerations look too big to even tell yourself the truth about your NO. So even if you think there is not a chance in hell that you can follow through with getting rid of the things, write them down.

Then, with each thing you write down, also write down all your fears and considerations about saying NO or letting go of or getting rid of them. You don't have to *do* anything about these things right now. Just write them down in a notebook. Write down the worst that can happen if you say NO. What is it you are most afraid of? Emptiness? Guilt? Being good to yourself?

Now write down some options. How can you create a gentle and firm NO to these things? Envision your life without these things. Does it frighten you? Make you feel bad, wrong, and guilty? Can you live in and with the emptiness?

EMPTINESS

NO is often the starting point of your path. And it takes courage to keep saying NO to what you don't want—until you find what you do want. In life we may be confronted with many choices. It's like being in a supermarket. Unless you pass by or say NO to a lot of stuff, there is not going to be any room for your YES. You need emptiness. There are way too many possibilities and distractions and things that can fill up your life.

Very often people are afraid to say NO because they are afraid of emptiness. They would rather have a bad relationship than no relationship. They would rather fill up the hole with false things or bad things than leave it empty. People are terrified of emptiness, space, and unlimitedness. Standing in emptiness takes another kind of courage, but emptiness is a tremendously powerful position.

I DON'T KNOW

Not I, not I, but the wind that blows through me.
—D.H. Lawrence,
Song of a Man Who Has Come Through

NOT KNOWING is extremely powerful. It is the *paper* in the rock-paper-scissors game—the empty canvas—the writer's blank piece of paper. There is nothing wrong with not knowing. It is the place of Possibilities. It is the Nothing out of which Creation happens. If NO is the Warrior Stance, NOT KNOWING is the Priest Stance, the closest to God. NOT KNOWING and silence are the objectives of mystics.

Every creation starts from emptiness. The empty stage must exist first. We must create the space for creativity to happen first. The line in *Field of Dreams* "If you build it, they will come" is about creating the space for something to happen. I have had students come to class, get up, and say, "I have nothing to do." Then they get present, and with whatever emotion or image that arises, they create amazing improvisations. Whole shows have been created that way in my classes. Many times in class when people *open* themselves to create and express, they exclaim afterward that they felt as if they had done nothing and had no idea where their inspiration came from. They surprise themselves. It is as if they are *channeling* creativity. Mother Theresa said, "I am the pencil. God does the writing."

I would say that most of what I do as a teacher is create the space for my students to create. Of course there are boundaries and limits, which make the space safe, but students thrive in the permission. I try to provide a bowl, rather than a box, for their genius to emerge and bloom and spill over.

The Four Principles themselves came out of NOT KNOWING. When I was first asked to teach at Playwrights Horizons Theatre School in Manhattan, I said that I thought it would be fun, but I didn't really know how or what I'd teach. To my surprise, the director of the school said that would be fine. She believed the students would benefit from being with me and from my experience. For a moment I thought I should read some books about acting before I began teaching. Then I thought, "I've been acting for years, have won a couple of prizes, been on Broadway, in movies, on TV. I don't read books. What do I do that works? What doesn't work?" I arrived at my first class open and not knowing exactly what I was going to do.

My teaching quickly settled upon The Four Principles and how to help students realize them. When the students did, their acting worked. I taught The Four Principles for twenty years, and they continue to become more powerful, surprising, and enlightening every day. They came from NOT KNOWING.

Because I have chosen never to tell students what work to do, they often must stand in NOT KNOWING until they find their own Commitments. It is difficult for many. They are so used to being told what to do that they have no idea what they want to do.

During a Dolphin Magic workshop that I conducted in the Florida Keys, Cynthia was working from the sensations in her body. She began to feel as if she were standing in the void. She was terrified of it. There was nothing there. It was pitch black. She panicked and felt as if she might die if she stayed there. With encouragement, she eventually accepted the void as a place where she would be able to create whatever she wanted. She began to see herself as a little creature wearing red sneakers racing all around the black void. In the image she was whooping, rolling, hollering, and having a great time. Eventually, she saw herself with a guitar, an easel, jewelry-making equipment—all sorts of fun things—but still no people. She was surprised, because in the past she had coped with her fear of emptiness by filling the void with other people, especially romantic relationships, when what she really needed was to be alone to create.

I talked with her some years after the workshop. She had become a fireball of creativity—writing new songs, and even performing in Nashville. Her life had become an expression of spontaneity and creativity. She got rid of both a relationship and a job that she didn't want, and now she is pursuing what she does want.

Sometimes it is valuable to consciously create Nothingness, especially when you find yourself going in the wrong direction. It is better to do nothing than to keep taking action that is antithetical to your true Commitment. So, when you feel yourself struggling or going in the wrong direction, STOP. You may want to fill the empty space. Don't. It is all right to not know. Don't fill the space with meaningless or harmful activity. Stop and Be Present.

In my first Broadway show I was a replacement two days before opening night. I had performed the part in Philadelphia, but not with anybody in the New York cast. The two rehearsals I was allotted were nightmares. The author-director was drunk and sometimes furious with the cast. It was such a crazy situation that, uncharacteristically, I almost walked out during the rehearsal on the day we were to open. Because it was such a critical day, I stayed.

Opening night was not going well. In the first act I felt stiff and tense. The second-act curtain went up. I was sitting on stage at a table. One other character was at the bar. I had the first line. Something in me said, "Stop!" So, I did. I didn't say my line. I just sat there looking out at the waiting audience feeling unbearably rigid. All I knew was just to stop—to stop the inauthenticity—to stop going in the wrong direction. I didn't know what to do about it. I just stopped. The hush in the audience deepened. I knew the other actor was wondering what the hell was going on. Nothing in me shifted, so I decided to say my line anyway. At that moment I opened my mouth to speak, in the back of the house the very drunk author said, "Ooooooeee. Somethin's gonna happen. I can tell. Somethin's gonna happen."

The whole situation was so absurd that the tension in my body broke. Here I was in my first Broadway show, having replaced another actress with just two days rehearsal, facing an audience of critics and a playwright who had just put me through hell in rehearsal. Suddenly, it seemed outrageously funny, and I relaxed completely.

Finding the humor in something certainly helps to break tension. The second act was not only great fun, but I have never read such universally good reviews for the whole show. But one of the best things I ever did for myself was to stop for that second or two.

I spent one summer in what I called The Space of NOT KNOWING. I had walked away from a dream—to start an artistic community. The project had started quite magically and then became more effortful and less effective as the months rolled by. I developed fierce headaches at every meeting. I should have listened to my body sooner, but I struggled because I felt guilty about letting down so many people. Finally, I announced that I needed a break and would not be at the meetings for a while. The whole thing collapsed. I'm clear that it was supposed to.

Soon after that my best friend died. I went into a time of emptiness and monumental grief—functioning just well enough to maintain myself bodily. I borrowed money to live on because I could teach only one class. I stopped in a big way. I was completely burned out.

Even so, I will always remember the summer as one of the most important summers of my life. As I sat on my deck slumped in sadness one day, I had a bizarre impulse to put up a tent in my back yard. I walked around my house looking for a flat spot on my rolling property. I found a nearly flat spot under some trees. It took me days to clean out the weeds and branches, dig up dirt from the streambed, and cart it to the tent site to even out the ground. I didn't really know why I was doing it. Was I crazy? A friend reassured me that Noah didn't know why he was building the ark, either. So I continued my work, stopping frequently to cry and grieve the loss of my dream and my best friend.

Finally, I put up my tent and furnished it. It was blue and white—the colors of the open sky, the colors of NOT KNOWING. Daily, I sat in my tent with my dogs and meditated, or I just sat. I didn't know what I wanted to do. I didn't know how I was going to live. The grief I felt seemed bottomless. I was in such a state of exhaustion that I thought I might die.

One day I was in my tent and it started to rain—hard. My two dogs were with me. I stretched out on my cushions and fell into a kind of trance. I could hear the rain, but I could not move. I dreamed that I was lying in the bottom of a rowboat that had drifted across a big lake. People on the pier were shouting at me to row back to them, but I couldn't move.

"God is going to have to pull the boat," I called to them, "I can't." Soon I felt the boat moving through the water, back toward the pier, but I was too exhausted to lift my head to see who was pulling the boat.

"You're going to have to sit up and steer," they shouted, "or you're going to crash into the shore!"

"God is going to have to turn the boat," I responded. "I cannot move." And I couldn't. At the last minute the boat turned and glided up to the dock. The people were amazed. They reached in and pulled me out. I woke up.

That dream was very important to me and to my developing trust in the Universe or God or whatever the mysterious energy is. For the rest of the summer I sat in NOT KNOWING, and I trusted it. I learned to honor my depression and my grief as a time of gestation and letting go. I came out of that summer feeling stronger and healthier than ever before.

Fear of emptiness is primal. Again and again I see people get close to emptiness and then start struggling to fill up the empty space. Being open takes great courage. If Nature abhors a vacuum, we humans are terrified of it. In our result-oriented world we struggle against NOT KNOWING. We take on false Commitments rather than wait for the real ones to emerge.

Don't force your heart to speak. "Hey! Waddya want! Come on! Come on! We gotta get going here!"

Knowing what you want and plowing ahead feels great. Accomplishing. Doing. Getting results. We all are programmed to admire and desire manifestation. In our *Do it!* culture, we do not tolerate space, emptiness, and NOT KNOWING well.

If we can learn to welcome emptiness as the Space for Creativity—like the Nothingness out of which the Big Bang happened, then we can cease struggling with it.

The empty times are very important to our development. We have to learn how to stop. Wait. Meditate. Go on vacation. Go for walks in the woods. Enjoy ourselves. Be calm. Let our hearts speak.

FALSE NOTHING

Some people are so dead to their desires that they really don't know what they want.

"Whaddya wanna do, Marty?" the guy asks his friend in the film *Marty*, written by Paddy Chayefsky.

"Nothin'," Marty answers with barely enough energy to speak. After a long pause, he adds, "Whadda *you* wanna do?"

Long pause. "I dunno. Nothin'."

That is not a true NOT KNOWING. It has an apathetic and dead quality. It is a result of suppressing the truth about what you want and don't want. I know the place. It is awful. I was so suppressed as a child that I didn't want anything. I didn't even want food. They used to beg me to eat. I was extremely thin. I used to be amazed that people actually *wanted* things. On the one hand, it was a defense: my mother could not punish me by taking anything away from me or not letting me do something, like go to the movies, because I didn't care enough for it to be a punishment. But not to care about anything at all is very painful. I envied people who wanted things. I used to pray to want something—just to want something. It has taken me a long time to become present enough to know what I want.

TRUE NOT KNOWING

True NOT KNOWING is not a dead feeling. It may be fearful, or awesome, or exciting, but it feels very alive. It is the space in which new things are created, like whole new universes. Therefore, embrace it. Welcome it. Allow it. Be in it. Surrender to it. How willing are you to stand in NOT KNOWING? Can you take breaks, or even stop all together? Do you meditate? Or do you fill all your time? How do you fill time and space? How are you in relation to silence? How about vacations? Are they active or quiet? Do you take breaks during your work day? Do you overeat? Do you have a television or radio playing even when you are not actively listening or watching? Are you able to physically relax? Are you a collector? Do you have too much stuff? Do you need to have people around you most of the time? Are you able to let go of people, places, and things? Or, do you hang on? How about your clothes closet? Attic? Garage? Store room? Desk?

Writers and artists often acknowledge their terror of the blank page and the empty canvas. But how on earth would they be able to create without it? Recently, during the holiday season, I spent the time that I wasn't engaged in those holiday activities cleaning out the Old and getting ready for the Unknown New. I cleaned out my closets and organized my house to the point where one day I felt complete. The holidays were over. My classes had not yet resumed. The media-touted Snow Storm of the Century virtually locked me in the house. For several days I had to hang out with the emptiness until I knew where I wanted to put my focus and energy. It was tough. A lot of feelings surfaced that had been covered. Perhaps it is our greatest fear of emptiness—that we will have to face ourselves and what we have suppressed in ourselves. However, once these feelings pass through us, our true desires will begin to surface.

I don't think the point of emptiness is to *stay* in emptiness. I think it is to create the space for one's true desires. We are human. We have our paths to travel. There is nothing wrong with desire. Our true desires are connected to our purpose in life. When we get rid of everything that is in the way, when we have the courage to stand in the emptiness and face the Void, the blank page, the empty stage, the desires can begin to emerge—perhaps first as shadows, as whispers, or as only the very next step.

KNOWING WHAT YOU WANT

It is all about wanting. —Neil Simon

Love/heart's desire/wanting is at the heart of great plays. It is also at the heart of great lives. Without it both plays and life are meaningless. Lack of desire will literally bore one to death in the theater and in life. Doing what you love is the position of manifestation. It is a very powerful position. It is the one that produces results. Some self-help books focus only on this position. When you know and *accept* what you want, envision, believe, love, desire, or need, the course of action is clear. It seems so easy. The power comes from being able to *tell the truth*. If there is no heart behind the doing, you will always miss the mark and feel unsatisfied.

Being committed cannot be taught because it is based on deeply personal feelings. Commitment can only be acknowledged. Many people lose touch with their ability to be committed because their true desires have been squelched and supplanted with what other people want them to want or what they think they're supposed to want.

The burden of trying to achieve what you are *supposed* to want is exhausting and crushing to the spirit. We come to believe that it is wrong to want what we want—that it is hopeless or silly or stupid. Often what we want or envision or desire or love frightens us. Our feelings are so powerful we want to suppress them. Our fear of not getting what we want *or* getting what we want prevents us from simply telling the truth. We'd rather be cool than reveal our hearts. Our desires make us vulnerable.

Commitment is like a car. A Rolls-Royce may look good, but if there is no fuel in the tank, it isn't gonna get there. Or the car can be a piece of junk, but as long as it works and has fuel, it will get there. One can fix it up, paint it, service it, but none of that will do any good whatsoever if there is no fuel. Vision, belief, love, desire, need are the fuel of Commitment.

"I love this part. I want to express it." An actor who loves acting, loves the part, loves the play and the production will do well—may even be brilliant. Some actors seem more naturally committed than others. Burt Lancaster was one of those actors who embodied an almost ferocious Commitment to whatever he did.

Commitment brings with it a kind of command that can overcome what some people would label lack of talent. An actor may not seem beautiful to you, graceful, expressive, or even interesting, but somehow his or her Commitment overcomes it all. Many actors work and have even become stars merely because of the quality of being committed.

Mike Nichols once said, "The premise is everything. Once you've got a great premise, you can make mistakes, and it will still work. If you don't have a good premise, you can do everything right, and it still won't work." Commitment is the premise.

One dynamic that is particularly important to note about Commitment is that the moment one commits barriers may pop up like ducks in a shooting gallery. For instance, you commit to finding a lover, and loneliness becomes more intense, incompatible people appear everywhere. Or you commit to expansion in business, and at first your business seems to contract.

Perhaps if one is wholeheartedly and fearlessly committed, the barriers do not present themselves. Rarely do we commit to something large or grand or seemingly difficult without some hesitation or fear. If one is prepared for this, then the barriers are not so utterly disheartening. Perhaps they are the Universe's way of testing the level of our Commitment or trust. At any rate, the greater the Commitment, the more likely rough area will need to be traversed.

One has only to look at weeds growing through cracks in cement—and ultimately breaking up the pavement to witness their Commitment to grow and move through the barriers. Weeds *will* grow, by god, and find the tiniest cracks in which to do so.

COMMITMENT BREEDS COMMITMENT

Commitment breeds Commitment. Love breeds love. Years ago I acquired a cat that I neither wanted nor loved. The upstairs neighbor was going to have him put to sleep because the cat was too vicious to be kept as a pet. I was incensed. I knew that because the neighbor had abused the cat, it had become ferocious, so I said I would take it. I was not happy about my decision. I could find nothing to love about this animal. He was a huge, black cat who weighed about seventeen pounds and was frighteningly fierce. However, my Commitment to his life was greater than my fear, so I kept him. His name, of all things, was Pansy.

He terrified me. I was embarrassed that I was keeping him. Everyone thought I was crazy. I didn't know what to do with him. I had to wear knee-high leather boots in my own apartment because he would attack my legs sometimes when I walked from room to room. I didn't kick him. I just stood there and watched him in a kind of awe and even admiration. His rage was awesome. I could feel the strength of his jaws and teeth through the leather of the boots. Fortunately, he didn't attack me above the boot line. Eventually, these boots were in shreds. I don't know when I no longer needed the boots, but over time he stopped attacking me, and I stopped wearing them.

I learned more about love and the miraculous possibility of healing from Pansy than from anyone or anything else. I learned that by just giving him the space to be and not punishing him for it, he healed. It took time. Simply through my Commitment to take care of him, feed him, and not abuse him, we came to love each other absolutely. It was slow. It took years. I remember when he first started coming to the door to greet me when I came home. He'd look at me. I'd look at him, and then he'd turn and walk away.

One night, after about a couple of years living with me, he jumped up on my bed as I was reading. I almost had a heart attack. I didn't know what he was going to do. I pretended to keep on reading. He stood there for a bit, and then jumped back off the bed. Eventually, over time, he came to sleep next to me, his head on my shoulder, his body stretched along mine. Often, in the night, purring loudly, he would touch my face gently with his paw and wake me up. It was as if he just needed to tell me how much he loved me.

When he was about seventeen years old, I lost him—literally—while driving from New York City to Washington, D.C. Unbeknownst to me, he jumped out of my car when I made a pit stop at a rest stop on the highway. I get sick to my stomach even now when I think about it.

When I arrived in Washington, D.C., he was not in the car. Because he liked to travel lying underneath the passenger seat and was quiet while I drove, I hadn't realized he was missing. I can still recall the sensations of terror when I realized he was not there.

My body felt instantly drained of all blood. I was supposed to start rehearsal, but I told the director I was going to look for my cat. If he wanted to fire me, fine, but I was going to look for him. For three days, in zero-degree weather, I drove up and down the turnpike, stopping at every gas station from Washington, D.C., to New York City, combing the area, calling for him. I hardly slept.

I was frantic with worry about him. I bargained with God. I knew I wasn't supposed to, but I did. "God," I said. "If you let me find my cat, I promise that I'll believe in you. I'll stop being an atheist and believe in you."

On the third day, I was out in the brambles beside a gas station, calling for him. I heard a cat. I tore through the underbrush looking for him. Finally, I saw a flash of a cat. It was not mine. I was sick with disappointment. My coat was ripped to ribbons, and my voice was gone. I knew I had to give up.

I got back into my car and drove up to the pump to fill it with gas.

A gas attendant came to the car. "That you yodelin' out there in the bushes?"

"Yeah," I answered. "I'm looking for my cat."

"Oh, we got a cat holed up in the tire room. Gray cat. You wanna see him?"

My cat was black, but I dragged myself out of the car and went with the guy into the tire room.

"He's in here somewhere," the guy said.

"Pansy?" I called out. I heard him yowl. It was a yowl of despair and rage and pain. I recognized the old demon's voice. The attendant and I pulled out tires, and I tore through them. Pansy wiggled through them and fairly leaped into my arms. He was gray—with dirt. By the way, the director did not fire me, but welcomed me back with open arms and was very happy for me. What, other than love, could have driven me to be so committed? Without question, the greater the Commitment, the greater the ability to get through the barriers, and the more willing one is to experience the discomfort.

MOVING THROUGH FEAR

I have heard it said that there are only two emotions: Love and Fear. I used to think that too simplistic. Now I'm beginning to think that there really is only one emotion: Love. When you strip away or express all the anger, grief, frustration, disgust, whatever— underneath it *all* is love. Fear covers Love. With this in mind, one can look at fear in a more friendly way: as the doorway showing you the room you need to enter.

Fear arises when the stakes are high—when love, desire, and need are present. If we don't deeply care about something, it doesn't seem to matter if we get it or don't get it. The mastery is to go for what we really want, confront the fear, let go of attachment to results, wear our desires like a loose garment, and trust the outcome as we proceed one step at a time.

Robert Fritz, founder of the D.M.A. training, uses a very interesting model when he talks about Commitment. It is based on an observation in folk physics that energy always moves along the path of least resistance. In nature, water goes where it is easiest to go. If it is blocked in one way, it will find another space in which to move. Fritz calls his model a tension-resolution system—a system whereby we find the path of least resistance. So, making a Commitment—saying what you want, or don't want, is tantamount to throwing a hook into the future attached to a rubber band. The desire hooks into the future and pulls you along toward it. When you have no conflict and the Commitment is wholehearted, it will resolve itself fairly quickly. "I want an apartment to share in New York City," a friend said. She had it within a week. Obviously, there was no conflict in that Commitment.

However, Fritz acknowledges that our Commitments often have what he calls "structural conflict." The simple example he uses is "I'm hungry; I want to eat" conflicted with "I'm overweight; I shouldn't eat." As Fritz states, "One property of structural conflict is that it is not resolvable, no matter what actions are taken." That doesn't stop us from *trying*, of course. His model is pretty depressing.

He uses a vivid analogy. Imagine standing in the center of a room. A rubber band is wrapped around you. One end of it is your Commitment, and it is attached to a wall in front of you. Let's say it is your Commitment to be a star. Unfortunately, the other end of the rubber band is a conflicting belief that it is wrong to show off, and that is attached to the wall behind you. Every time you try to move toward your desire to be a star, the tension of the belief that it is wrong to show off increases until eventually you are pulled back to the center of the room. The closer you get to your goal, the more force is exerted by the opposing rubber band. ("I want to be a star; it's wrong to show off.") Eventually, you have to give up because you are worn out. No matter how many times you try, you *always* fail.

As if that were not discouraging enough, it gets worse. We try various solutions to resolve the structural conflict. We try to change the dominant belief into "It is okay to show off." Fritz says that then all the energy goes into changing your belief, so you still don't get what you want. The other solution is to give up your desires—which may lead to a kind of peace, but you still don't have what you want.

So we deal with our desires through three strategies: 1. Not attempt much. 2. Negative reinforcement. (I hate myself or someone will be mean to me if I don't do it.) 3. Assert our will through positive thinking. Fritz makes a clear case showing how the strategies do not work—or work up to a point and then disintegrate, sometimes leaving you even farther from your goal.

Fortunately, Fritz doesn't leave you there. He does offer a solution. Essentially, he says that the solution to structural conflict is to create "structural tension." "Structural tension has two components: vision and reality." "Vision" and "reality" are other ways of saying Commitment and Being Present. Essentially, the way to a goal is by keeping a focus on the vision (Commitment) and staying in touch with what current reality is. Where do you want to go, and where are you now?

In my experience, it is not only conflicting beliefs that hold us back, but also what *is unconscious and unexperienced* that holds us back.

The good news is you can access the information and unhook the rubber bands that hold you back by experiencing the barriers physically as they come up in the process toward the realization of your Commitments. I think there's a kind of cosmic joke: the End *is* really the Means. We think what we want is a career, or a job, or a relationship, and that if we get our heart's desire, we'll be happy. If we climb Mount Everest, we'll feel good. If we just get to the top, we won't feel the way we do now. *What we don't realize is that the real goodies in life are in the trip.*

I've seen actors endure hardships, experience emotions and sensations that are horrendously difficult because they are in a *movie*. They wouldn't consider doing such things in everyday life, but because they're so happy to be in a movie they will endure much. And that is good. It is the growth that happens in our climb toward our goals that is perhaps the greatest value. "Process is all," I once heard Mike Nichols say.

So as you move closer toward your goals, the pressure of the unconscious and unexperienced sensations will be felt more and more. If you allow them to become conscious by Being Present in the Body, then it is as if the hook into the past snaps, and the rubber band relaxes: you can move forward more easily. The closer you get to absolute love the deeper the barriers.

Commitment is not possible without passion, desire, need, fervency, love, hunger. And these things are not possible without arousing fear, which is to be welcomed and to be embraced. People waste so much energy trying to get rid of fear. Be afraid. It is the flag that demonstrates caring. It is the badge of courage. It is very frightening to tell yourself and others the truth about what you really want and what your heart's desire is.

The difficult thing to master about Commitment is just telling the truth, letting it be, and taking steps on your path. It means giving yourself the space to be where you are and not trying to be where someone else is. If you see someone in great activity moving forward with great speed while you are standing in NOT KNOWING, stay where you are. Or, if you're saying NO to things using all your strength to get rid of what doesn't work in your life, don't expect to stand in the stillness of NOT KNOWING.

Sometimes we must switch back and forth from one to the other rapidly. No, no, no, no, well, let's stop for a minute, hmmmm, take a break, hey what about—? Yeah, that's it, do it now!

PHASES OF COMMITMENT

There are four phases in Commitment: Starting, Maintenance, Completion, and Rest. They are the spring, summer, fall, and winter of Commitment. Each day, each activity, each yoga pose, each thing we do is composed of these four phases—from writing or acting in a play, to cooking dinner. Each phase brings with it the need for a different kind of mastery.

I have difficulty with *all* phases of Commitment. My first play, *Juno's Swans*, was finally being produced at the Second Stage Theatre in New York City. It had been a ten-year process that had been excruciating at moments. I had been through a lot of pain with it. I had learned a lot. I had done nearly twenty rewrites. At one point I turned to my wonderful director, Marsha Mason, and said, "Well, if I could only get the beginning, the middle, and the end, I'll have a play."

STARTING

Spring. Beginnings can be very exciting or scary. Personally, I find starting difficult. The whole process of getting to and through a first rehearsal is painful for me. Opening nights are nerve-wracking. It is no accident that I created a workshop *to release the energy to start on your heart's path, and keep going.*

In physics, the law of inertia states a body at rest tends to stay at rest, and a body in motion tends to stay in motion. Starting requires energy. Suppressing fear *uses* energy. Granted, it is easier to start if there is no fear or dread. However, it is still possible to find the energy for starting if one does not use one's energy in suppressing or trying to control fear.

I had the mistaken idea that one should begin like a racehorse springing out of the gate at the starting bell. I thought starting was painful like birth.

When I was fifty, I decided to learn to ski. I am scared of height, speed, and feeling out-of-control. I figured skiing would pretty much help me confront all three fears. I told my instructor at the first lesson how scared I was. He put my boot in my right ski. "Can you move it back and forth?" Well, of course, I could do that, silly man. (Smart man.)

By the end of that hour I was skiing down the bunny trail. He taught me that when starting something scary, to do it very, very easily. If you can experience your fear, take a simple, easy step, and keep taking simple, easy steps, you are started and moving forward before you know it. Once something is going, it takes less energy to keep it in motion.

Racehorses have to warm up. They don't just start at the starting gate. I use something I call the Fifteen-minute Solution. I set the timer on my phone for fifteen minutes and do the thing I've been resisting or dreading. Usually I keep going, but I give myself permission to stop if I don't want to continue. Getting started can be hard.

MAINTENANCE

Summer. A routine, knowing what you are doing day by day, being committed to a project, can be a happy time. But doing something like the same show eight times a week month after month can turn to drudgery, boredom, ordinariness, dullness, the dog days of summer.

Maintenance is the endurance test, the long haul. In my first professional play in New York, *The Trojan Women*, I asked the distinguished actress Mildred Dunnock what was the one thing I needed in order to be a successful actress. With no hesitation she answered, "Endurance." I didn't like the answer at the time, but I never forgot it. I understand more what she meant now, and I accept it.

The desire to quit may be very strong somewhere in the middle. A great deal of soul-searching is required to find out if the end result is still something that you want, believe in, or desire. It is important not to lie to yourself just because the going gets rough.

Probably we all have an impulse to stop somewhere in the middle. My point seems to be when I am about seven-eighths done. Seven-eighths of the way through a project, I feel my energy sag, and I want to quit. If I can just keep going, I will have an energy surge and get to the end. Do you know where your impulse to quit happens?

Perseverance counts, but some of us are trained to keep going no matter what, even when we *should* quit, even when we are no longer on the path with heart. Other people quit so readily that they never finish anything. It is only through Being Present that you will know the real truth about the situation.

If you don't quit, if you stay present, trust, and get a little help from your friends, if you stay the course, you will eventually arrive at:

COMPLETION

Fall. Letting go. Completion is a kind of death. Being able to complete things means a kind of willingness to face dying and grief. For some people it is virtually impossible. They will get right up to the very last second and then not complete it. Contractors in my house have left the strangest little details unfinished.

I seem more comfortable when it comes to completion. So when I renovated my house recently, I didn't chase after the workmen. I just finished the details myself. It isn't that hard to screw a wall plate back on an electrical outlet, but experiencing the completion of the job *is*. God knows how many unfinished plays, symphonies, novels, short stories, songs, and needlepoint are lying around the world not finished because their creators could not confront the feeling of completion.

When I taught in a semester format, I learned to use the last day to help my students master completion as consciously as possible. I did that because there was a lot of craziness that would happen as classes drew to a close. One girl always became disruptive during the last class and picked a fight. She lashed out almost uncontrollably. When I spoke with her about it, she acknowledged that completions were always messy for her. She had never finished a relationship or an experience in serenity. The only way she had dealt with completion in the past was to suppress her emotions and then explode. The next semester I gave her and everyone else an opportunity to actually express feelings about completing the last class. She burst into sobs and cried so hard tears splashed on her dress. Her grief was much easier to be with.

Letting go is surrender. It is good-bye. Celebration is a healthy way to ease the process of completion. Closing-night parties may be sad, but they help with this process of completion. The fall colors are wildly celebratory in the process of letting go.

Isolation makes celebration difficult. Try not to be alone during the completion phase. Each day, each activity, each class, each audition, each show presents the need for celebration. It is difficult to find ways to celebrate that don't include overeating and drinking. But I do find that just being with people I love and sharing my love with them works. Going out with a cast after a show or after a day's shoot has the kind of camaraderie of soldiers after a battle. We made it through! Actors are great to play with. There is such a sense of relief and joy and sharing.

I am almost always restless after a show. The better the performance, the greater my restlessness. A good celebration prepares us for Rest.

REST

Winter. Rest is an important phase in Commitment that we often ignore, leave out, or deny ourselves. If the celebration is complete, then the actual Rest is more acceptable. Stillness can be difficult for people. It requires the ability to empty out and to just *be*. It is the time of deep healing and rejuvenating, of withdrawing and spirituality. People are often surprised at the depression that follows a great task, the post-partum blues. "Why am I not happy?" they wonder. "I did a great thing. I'm happy with the results, but I'm depressed." Winter is the time of gestation. It is not that nothing is happening. Trust rest. Trust stillness. It is another kind of emptiness that will be filled.

AUTHENTIC COMMITMENT

So much of drama is about Commitment and what is in the way of it. Not being in touch with one's Commitment is the problem that forms many characters in literature: Hamlet's torturous route to the fulfillment of the Commitment to his father's ghost to kill Claudius. Many plays are about the characters discovering their Commitment: Rosalind discovers her love for Orlando, and follows it all the way to marriage at the end.

These are questions an actor must look at when studying a character: What does this character love, desire, want, and need? What is it that the character does *not* want? Is there any conflict? Does the character lie to himself about it? What barriers is this character facing? What is spoken? Unspoken?

Ask the same questions of yourself: What do you really love, desire, want, and need? What is it that you do *not* want? What doesn't work for you in your life? Is there any conflict? Do you lie to yourself about it? What barriers are you facing? What is spoken? Unspoken?

Telling the truth about your Commitment is the hardest part. Taking a step along the path toward it is the next hardest part. How much safer it is to go through life with our hearts shut down pursuing what we don't care about because it does not bring up any particularly strong feelings.

There is no way to be committed without Being Present. You have to be with all your feelings. You have to show up. You have to *be there* both in physical space and in your physical body. Otherwise, there is no Commitment. Therefore, the effort that we think we must spend to get committed or drive ourselves or become motivated actually must go toward just Being Present—just showing up.

My authentic Commitments have been humble. I am not ambitious. Sure, there was a part of me that has urged me to try to write the Great American Novel/Screenplay and Save the World while being thin and beautiful, but that's the part that felt it could not be loved until I did those things. What I have really wanted and needed was to heal myself. Like my cat Pansy, I needed a safe place to feel and express all my rage and despair and craziness. Thank God I found acting and the theater. It gave me such a space. For whatever reason, I didn't need to be a star.

I needed sanctuary. I needed to create that kind of home for myself, and I have. I thought I created it for the stray dogs that I found, but they didn't really *need* a fireplace in the bedroom and a deck with a hot tub. I do not have a luxury home, not by any means. Its style is something I call Exxon Moderne, but I love it. I love my hammock in the living room, the drapes that I put on the *outside* of my house and all the many things that I have hammered and sewn to make it my own Paradise Spa and Health Resort. I love sitting here writing with a fire in the fireplace, glancing out the window now and then at the birds in the bird feeder, and the huge crows in the tree waiting for the handful of dry dog food that I toss to them. I love seeing deer in my yard, watching the chipmunks, and seeing four raccoons on my deck at dusk. They are things I never knew as a child growing up in a house I hated, crowded next to other houses with tiny yards.

Obviously, I have been committed to my pets.

I love teaching. It is thrilling to me. I am in awe of my own students. They have taught me to love people. They surprise, astonish, amuse, delight, impress me, and then golly, pay me. I am committed to them and to their creativity. I am committed to creativity—all kinds—any kind. Creativity to me is miraculous. Creativity puts me in touch with God as no religion or church has ever done. God is, indeed, the Creator. As a student recently put it, "Creativity is one-stop shopping."

All of my Commitments are astonishingly wonderful to me, if humble. They have all come from my authentic need to heal myself, to open my heart, to love myself, others, life, and God. It has been underlying it all. And I have gone one step at a time dealing with what is right in front of my nose, like Stephen King, who responded when asked how he was able to write so many books, "One word at a time."

What I have noticed is that following my true Commitments is how I have contributed to others. What I learned through acting is what I've been able to teach. In the home sanctuary that I created, I have had dozens of workshops. Many people have come here and shared the space that I created.

If you really want to contribute to the world, follow your authentic heart's desires. Initially, if you are changing direction, you may find people upset, but eventually, even they will benefit from your being true to yourself.

Take a moment to acknowledge what it is at this time that you authentically want, need, and desire. Better yet: *write it all down*. You may find yourself discouraged about the list even before you create it, but just write it down as soon as you finish reading this. Write down what is authentic for you at this time. Write it down *no matter what your mind is telling you right now*. Write down at least one thing. Or, at the least, say it to yourself right now.

You might start with what you need to say NO to. What is it you need to get rid of? Have you gotten rid of things that don't work in your life or are you at the end of a project and standing in emptiness? What is your YES? What are you doing that you enjoy doing? What do you want to do more of? What do you need? What is your priority now? Remember that Commitments are not things that are written in stone or have to be heavy. Tell the truth. That's the hard part.

SUMMARY

Commitment is telling the truth about what you want, need, love, desire, are drawn to, turns you on, and then, taking action. Commitment has three positions: NO; I DON'T KNOW; and YES. There are four phases in Commitment: Starting, Maintaining, Completing, Rest.

COMMUNICATION

*You walk in the room, you plant your feet, you
look the guy in the eye, and you tell the truth.*
—James Cagney

Communication is the Alpha and the Omega of The Four
Principles. Acting *is* Communication. It is what I call the
Fail Safe Principle. It is the hook that opens your parachute
when you can't find the rip cord. Communication is both the goal
and the life preserver. In terms of The Four Principles, it is the life
line. If you *know* what your Commitment is, communicate it. If you
don't know what your Commitment is, can't Be Present with the
sensations in your body, and are unable to relax, start
communicating about that. Either way, communicate. "To be or
not to be. That is the question." Hamlet starts from not knowing
what to do. Throughout the play, he works through his doubts and
fears communicating with the audience as listener until he arrives at
a clear action, "The play's the thing wherein I'll catch the
conscience of the King!"

Communication saves you if you're an actor. It saves you in life.
It is what starts you on the path of your heart's desires. It is what
gets you there. Communication is all about movement. Good

Communication moves everything forward, and movement is what The Four Principles are all about.

In August Strindberg's play *The Stronger* there are only two women characters. One does all the talking. One does all the listening. Who is the stronger, the speaker or the listener? There are many actors who will swear that the secret to acting is all about listening—that in fact, listening is their only aim when acting—to listen and react. To them, acting equals reacting. Actors who truly listen are generous and very easy to work with.

Good directors, like good leaders, are great listeners. They are your audience during rehearsal. A good one doesn't judge what you do so much as respond to what you do. Mike Nichols was like that. Mike saw me in an Off Broadway play. Shortly afterward his secretary called and asked me if I would be willing to participate in a reading of a screenplay for him. My heart rate sped up wildly. "Ummm, sure!" I tried to sound casual. Meryl Streep would read her role. Kurt Russell would read his role. The authors, the producers, and Mike Nichols, whom I did not know but idolized from afar, were going to be in the room. The secretary told me I would read *all* the other female roles, including Cher's. "Great!" I said, sitting down before I fainted. When I got the script, so much of it was underlined in red that I nearly panicked. I couldn't believe how much I was going to be reading. I was so nervous I did not sleep the night before.

At the reading, before we began, Meryl Streep, whom I had never met, came up to me and said, "I'm really nervous!" I was so grateful I grabbed her and hugged her. "Thank you. Thank you for saying that. Me, too. Me, too." Meryl's Communication helped. We sat down at the table and read. Mike Nichols giggled appreciatively at my first line, which relaxed me completely. I had fun. He is a great listener.

After the reading, the authors insisted that Mike give me a role even though none was really right for me. That's how I ended up in my first movie—pretty amazing for a woman who hadn't taken an acting class until the age of twenty-seven, had no contacts, never lived in Los Angeles, and was a scaredy-cat to boot. The film was *Silkwood*.

Communication is a two-way street: speaking and listening are equally powerful. Years ago, I was so lucky to be cast as Toby Landau in a touring production of *The Gingerbread Lady* by Neil

Simon, directed by Anthony Perkins, and starring Maureen Stapleton. Tony was a wonderful director, Maureen was amazing, and the others in the cast were excellent. I was having a grand time.

One night we were performing in a tent theater-in-the-round. There was a terrible storm. The rain sounded like drums beating on the tent. As Maureen and I stood at the top of the aisle to make our entrance, we realized the audience could not hear the actors because of the drumming rain. The three microphones hanging over the stage did not help.

Maureen grabbed my wrist. "Screw the blocking," she hissed. "Head for the microphone and just speak right into it." I did exactly as she told me. I walked on stage, did not go where I was supposed to go, went underneath one microphone, and literally shouted the lines of my long monologue directly into it. I felt absurd, but at the end of my monologue the audience stood up and cheered. It wasn't my acting. It wasn't how good I was. It was just that that they were so happy to hear me.

It was a great lesson. The first rule of theater is to be heard. Communicate. We need to speak up and be heard.

No endeavor, no relationship, and no performance is ever dead as long as there is Communication. You may not have a clue as to why you are there, or what you are doing, or why you are doing it, or what you think or feel. Nevertheless, if you reach out to communicate, you will get through. It is important to communicate even if you're not clear about what to say:

"We need to talk."

"What about?"

"I don't know. Something doesn't feel right."

And you're off and running.

One time I agreed to do a reading of a play. The author was a personal friend, so I broke one of my cardinal rules that I must read a play before I agree to do it. An actress had dropped out of the play at the last minute, so I was only able to read it just before the reading was scheduled. To my dismay, I didn't understand the play at all. I knew it was English, but it didn't make any sense to me. It was obscure. I didn't know what it was about. I was horrified. What to do? Well, I thought, I'm just going to communicate the hell out of this play. Throw it out there like I know what I'm talking about.

Later, the playwright was very pleased with what I had done in the reading. Several people in the audience came up to me and said,

"You were wonderful. Um—" a quick glance to check that the author wasn't listening, "What was this play about?" They gasped in amazement when I smiled and shrugged, "I don't know. I haven't a clue."

Obviously, Communication is not just verbal. Musical expression has great power. It reaches in and communicates directly to the heart and soul, bringing people together who do not even speak the same language. During the Cultural Revolution in China, all Western instruments were forbidden. Possession of a violin could get a person thrown into jail. In a documentary *From Mao to Mozart,* Isaac Stern is in China to teach music after the restrictions were relaxed. The Communication between him and his students is breathtaking. He plays and looks right into the eyes of his students. Emotions play all over his face as he speaks with his violin teaching them how to express fully through music. The love and compassion and healing in this documentary are deeply moving. Music elicits every human emotion. It communicates deeply.

There is a wonderful documentary about Maria Callas in which Franco Zeffirelli talks about what made her so beloved by her audiences. He said it was that her desire to communicate always triumphed over any emotion that threatened to overcome her. She sang on the edge. But no matter how powerful the emotions she was feeling, she always pushed through to communicate. In Zeffirelli's words, "She was heroic."

People who want power do whatever they can to control Communication. In war, the first thing to do is take control of Communication by listening to the enemy's communications, breaking their secret codes, cutting off their ability to communicate with one another, taking over the radio stations, and doing whatever it takes to be in charge of Communication. If you can take control of Communication, the war is all but won. If you lose your ability to communicate, it is all but lost.

The Internet, which has changed the world and is something never dreamed of by science fiction writers, is creating the space for all people to communicate with one another freely and immediately. As a result, there are people who want to take control of the Internet. So far, it has been difficult for any one to do that. Power to the People, indeed.

NON-COMMUNICATION

To really get the power of Communication, let's look at the effects of non-communication. Non-communication is the last defense of the powerless and is, therefore, a form of attack. Children can and do drive their parents crazy by refusing to communicate. I know. I used it with my mother a lot. It is the one thing children can do to defend themselves and attack their parents.

Parents get frustrated by sullen children who will not speak. Directors and playwrights also get frustrated with actors who do not communicate, who seem more interested in examining their own navels or thoughts or emotions and who mutter or can't be heard. Sometimes actors are afraid of feeling intense emotions for fear of seeming self-indulgent. Hear ye, hear ye, all actors who read this: *There is no feeling that is self-indulgent, there is only not communicating that makes you* appear *self-indulgent.* The same goes for you actors on the stage of life. As long as your thrust is toward Communication, you will never seem self-indulgent.

How many times have there been scenes in movies like this:

"Where are the rest of your men?"

"All I have to tell you is my name, rank, and serial number, bub!" And the hero stays silent no matter how much they torture him (at least in the movies.) In his silence is his heroism. The guy who talks is labeled a coward. The guy who "sings" is a traitor.

In our personal relationships, not communicating can also be an attack. If you want to end a relationship, don't communicate. That'll do it for sure. Once people stop communicating with one another they might as well end the relationship right there because it is over. It is a dead, done thing. Bury it. Of course, we are communicating all the time, whether openly or not. Non-communication is unspoken communication: "I don't want a relationship with you. I want to stop this—whatever it is."

Imposing non-communication on someone is one of the worst punishments meted out to a prisoner. Solitary confinement—being in the "hole," as they say in the movies, can drive a person crazy. Other prisoners congratulate a guy coming out of solitary confinement if he can still make a coherent sentence. Non-communication serves a lot of painful purposes: attack, defense, and punishment.

Lying, withholding the truth, "making nice," is another form of non-communication. Lies are negative Communication. Like drugs, lies may work for a while; but eventually, they catch up and slam us upside the head fast and hard. Lying creates expensive messes that other people end up having to clean up. It saddens me when our own leaders and our own presidents so baldly lie to us.

One of the striking characteristics of insanity is an inability to communicate well or at all. Not communicating makes an actor look insane. One time in class, a man did a monologue. For some reason, he never once looked at his partner. He looked down at the floor, up at the ceiling, everywhere but at his partner. He was speaking English, but neither I nor anyone else could understand what he was saying. He looked really crazy. He sounded insane. I had him do it again and asked him to look his partner in the eye without looking away—to communicate to that person directly. It was pretty amazing. Suddenly, everyone in the room could understand what he was saying, and he no longer seemed insane. In fact, his character *wasn't* insane. The actor was even surprised to find out that he had seemed crazy. It wasn't his intention to make his character insane. It was simply his non-communication that made him appear so out of his mind.

A young man who had studied with me briefly called me and started ranting and raving about the world situation, the water, what his voices were telling him. It was a bit scary. He was irrational, but I didn't engage with his mind. It would have gone on forever. Instead, I asked him to tell me what was going on in his body. It was difficult. He didn't want to go there, because he didn't want to feel what he was feeling. But he knew me. He knew the drill. On some level that was why he called me—to get help to Be Present. He had an immense amount of fear. Wild fear. At first, he could only tell me that he was hunched against the wall on his bed, smoking cigarettes. Firmly, but gently, I asked him to go into his body. He was resistant at first, but finally he began to feel his fear and to tell me what it felt like. In a very short time, he calmed down and sounded rational again. Perhaps insanity, or much of what passes for insanity, is an inability to Be Present in the body, accept the sensations, and communicate about it to someone.

I have had students who have been diagnosed as mentally ill who have benefited tremendously from learning how to be in their bodies, accept the sensations, and communicate. God knows the acting profession attracts those of us who are wounded, highly sensitive, and misunderstood. I have seen people move through extremely intense emotions by learning how to experience them consciously and stay in Communication. So much release, so much healing happens when one is able to do that. Unfortunately, we live in a culture that fears feelings and sensations. People run away from intense emotions in themselves and others. They try to run away, fix, change, and drug, rather than be with emotions with trust and compassion.

I had a student who was a wonderful writer and actor. He had a lot of fear. One time he had a panic attack. At one point, it got so intense that his whole body went rigid. I wasn't alarmed so long as he stayed in Communication with me. He did. The panic passed, and he was calm afterward. Unfortunately, he didn't stay with the process, and dropped out of class.

Some time later, he called me. Apparently, he had had another panic attack in a therapist's office. To his great surprise, she left the office for a moment, called the police, and had him put into a mental hospital. They came and got him and took him away. He was shocked by it all. He thought he was just afraid and that she would help him through his fear. Instead, she and the people at the hospital told him he was insane. Now he has that label to contend with, and unfortunately, believes it. I know what I am saying flies against convention. However, I have seen it happen with so many of my acting students that no matter how intense their emotions are, as long as they can stay present with them and stay in Communication, there is a great deal of hope for natural healing. Being able to communicate is a manifestation of health and sanity.

Basically, non-communication will stop you dead in your tracks. Nothing moves unless there is Communication. Something as simple as an unanswered phone call will take the steam out of forward locomotion. Is it becoming clear that each of The Four Principles is about creating movement toward your heart's desires? If you understand this, you will devote yourself to Communication, knowing that it is the fuel that moves things forward.

LASER COMMUNICATION

Often inexperienced actors don't communicate powerfully. Their voices become small or restricted. They don't look at the other actors. They look down, up, away—any place other than in actual contact with people's eyes. The more powerful their feelings and emotions, the more they don't want to communicate. Not looking someone in the eye—not communicating—is an attempt to control emotions. When actors *do* communicate, their emotions become even more intense, so they may squiggle, squirm, turn away, back into the wall, and squint their eyes shut if they haven't learned to be fully present with uncomfortable feelings. I am not exaggerating. As a teacher, I hate to leave people in a place where they have not communicated, because it leaves them stuck in their emotions. The emotions have no place to move. Communication is locomotion/loco*emotion.* Communication moves the emotions.

So I tell the ones who don't communicate to look the other actor in the eyes while speaking and to not look away at all. I call it Laser Communication. "Don't worry about acting. I know it will seem unnatural and terribly uncomfortable, but just do it as an experiment," I say. That is very difficult for some people. They automatically look away in order to regroup or recover. When students don't allow themselves to look away even for a second, wonderful things begin to happen in their work.

This may sound absurdly simple, but watch great actors. They communicate directly with their eyes. It is as James Cagney said, "You walk in the room, you plant your feet, you look the guy in the eye, and you tell the truth."

While making a film, Glenn Ford was having great difficulty with a love scene. It was not working. After many attempts, the director finally told him to just look the woman in the eyes and say the words. The scene worked.

When actors use Laser Communication, they are not just putting out energy, but receiving it. The eyes have it. In film much of the focus is on the eyes of actors. During close-ups, when the camera is solely on you, most actors to whom you are speaking will stand right next to the camera even if they are not being filmed and do the scene with you, looking right at you. The difference between speaking to a person and speaking into a blank space is so noticeable in the eyes that this practice is universal. Laser Communication includes reacting and receiving, as well as speaking and projecting.

Watching people struggle against Communication makes it clear why they do not communicate: it is to save themselves from feeling.

We have all kinds of excuses. We think we want to protect another person. We don't want to hurt them. We don't want to upset them and cause them pain. These are lies we tell ourselves no matter how well-constructed and reasonable they seem. The reason we don't communicate is that we cannot stand the pain it causes *us*. We are protecting only ourselves. It takes courage to communicate—great courage.

As simple as this key to authentic acting is, it enhances all the principles—which is why I call Communication the Fail Safe Principle. When actors use Laser Communication, it forces them to Be Present. When actors use Laser Communication, it teaches them what their characters truly want and are committed to. When actors use Laser Communication, it makes them appear much more relaxed, confident, and self-assured. Love scenes become more believable because lovers look deeply into one another's eyes. Some actors may argue that it is *natural* to look away. "Yeah," I say, "But it is only great acting when it is a *choice*—not an automatic response—to show that the character is afraid, sullen, shy, or lying."

People who don't look you in the eye tend to look self-indulgent, self-concerned, self-centered, and self-conscious. It is not a pretty image or one that one wants to project in life. It is unpleasant to be with someone who doesn't look at you when speaking or look at you when listening. It makes you feel unimportant.

For several years I had an agent who didn't look me in the eye. Once, when I was in a restaurant with him I wanted to scream, "Look at me!" I didn't, but I was very uncomfortable with him. He was always looking over my shoulder as if to see who else was coming in the door. It made me feel like he was looking for someone more important to him. We parted ways. He went to California.

Many years later I ran into him again—in the same restaurant. He asked me to sit down for a moment and chat. I was shocked. He was looking me right in the eye and talking to me. He didn't once look over my shoulder. He was really present with me and seemed interested in what I was saying. He was completely transformed. After a short time I couldn't help but comment. "Bob!" I exclaimed. "You seem so different. You're...well...*here*. What have you been doing?" I thought maybe he had been in some very effective therapy. He answered, "I got AIDS."

"Oh," I said. "Oh."

He'd been slammed upside the head by life, and he woke up.

Some time afterward I heard he had died. I was grateful that he had some time to really be here while he was alive.

Looking the guy in the eye works in acting, and assuredly, it works in life, too. The results of Laser Communication are quite amazing. If you want to appear confident and self-assured, practice Laser Communication on job interviews or business meetings and watch the result. If you want to be a great lover, look him or her right in the eye. How much do you look your wife, husband, son, child, or friend in the eye? If you do, I guarantee they will feel more loved and cared for by you.

In class, I usually must teach new students about Laser Communication. After that, I have to remind them only occasionally. It doesn't take much time to learn the importance of Laser Communication. Once students see what happens when an actor who hasn't been communicating uses Laser Communication, they get it.

That doesn't mean it is easy. It is still hard to do because Communication demands an ability and willingness and courage to feel. There is no escaping it. The Four Principles are connected.

COMMUNICATING TO GROUPS

Laser Communication works in groups as well. As an actor, I love playing roles in which I speak directly to the audience. I love the reactions and energetic interplay that happens. Years ago I saw Pauline Collins in a one-woman play called *Shirley Valentine* in which she spoke directly to the audience. She made the audience fall in love with her in about fifteen seconds. When a man coughed softly in the audience, she looked in his direction and spoke her next line. Pauline Collins was listening to the audience. Immediately, the audience knew that she knew we were there. Her acknowledgment of us made us feel loved, so we loved her in return. She did what I tell my students: *reward response*. By being very aware of response, even a small response, you are Laser Communicating. Some performers have another way of putting it: they call it working the room, getting into an energetic connection with the audience and making them part of your experience. That requires a kind of hyper-listening and responding.

There is no performance without an audience. There is no Communication without a listener. Shakespeare, the Great Communicator, created for himself the most brilliant context a writer could have: a totally non-judgmental, ready-to-listen audience, an audience to whom he could tell anything and everything without censorship or shame. He was fearless in the area of Communication. He told the whole truth, withholding nothing. All his characters are willing to reveal everything about themselves to the audience. It was as if he believed there was nothing he could not say to an audience. In *Richard III*, Act I, Scene 2, Richard approaches the audience and asks, "Was ever woman in this humour woo'd? Was ever woman in this humour won?" And he proceeds to divulge to the audience his evil plans and outrageous behavior, taking them into his confidence and assuming the audience will understand him perfectly, even approve. To Shakespeare, an audience was safe. They were the non-judging listener.

I agree with Shakespeare. An audience by its very nature is willing to listen, ready to be entertained, and even to forgive. One time I was in a play and not doing very well. I could feel the audience was not really with me. In the second act, I somehow became present, and the audience just as immediately connected with me, forgetting and forgiving me for the first act.

An audience actually teaches me what the play and the character are really about by their reactions. It was the honest reaction of the audience that taught me about acting in *Cloud 9*. Strangely, audiences have no idea what an effect they have on a play. Often they believe they have no effect and are invisible and inaudible. That, perhaps, is what makes them so honest. Sometimes they talk out loud, unaware that actors can hear them. Perhaps they have spent too much time in front of a television. I wish audiences knew how important they are, how much of an effect they have.

I may have uncertainties about my talent as an actor, but I know one thing for sure: I'm a great listener. Producers should pay me to come to opening nights. I am a natural audience cheerleader. In my own career on stage, I have noticed that an audience can become highly responsive if there are at least three or four cheerleaders in the house, people who are good responders. A responsive audience energizes actors. It is a cyclical energy booster.

Unless there is an audience, there is no show. Unless there are spectators, there are no Olympics. Unless there is a customer, there is no sale. Unless there is a listener, what one says has no impact. Unless a tree is heard falling, what does it matter if it makes a sound or not? Who is your audience in life? Have you created non-judgmental listeners?

A woman who was not an actress took my acting class for a while. She joined in wholeheartedly. She went on to a career in travel and called me to let me know that she had been called upon to speak before many groups and had used what she had learned about communication to great benefit. She was having a lot of fun, and she was very successful. If you have any occasion in which you need to speak to a group, assume that they are friendly and willing to hear what you have to say. Speak from your passion and your truth, and you will be amazed at your reception.

TELLING THE TRUTH

"You look the guy in the eye, and *you tell the truth.*" Cagney was right. Authentic acting is not about pretending. The writers supply the words; the actors supply the true feelings beneath them. Great acting, like great writing, gets as close to the truth as is possible. Like the old adage "truth in advertising," truth in art is what works. It is the foundation of great art.

Communication is about telling the truth—sometimes a very uncomfortable truth. It is heroic to communicate the truth. Humans have a primal fear of telling the truth. The strong drive not to communicate may be both protective and culturally trained. There is a prevailing belief that if we tell the truth, we will be hurt. We fear that if we tell the truth, we will be killed for it or punished for it. Some of history corroborates this, which is why truth-tellers seem so brave, so courageous. They are. In my observation, acting has evolved in terms of truth-telling. The emotional depth actors go to in order to get to the truth of their characters is astounding. Losing weight, gaining weight, exploring all aspects of being a human being—acting has become a kind of extreme sport of truth seeking.

If we are agitated, angry, or upset, we probably will find it difficult to communicate honestly. Do not confuse attacking or defending with telling the truth. Attacking someone—no matter how truthful you think you are being—is just attack. The real truth would be, "I want to attack you. I want to blame you. I want to justify myself. I want to defend myself. I want to declare how righteous I am about the situation. I want to make you wrong." That's what the real truth would be. Any sentence that focuses on the other person "You said, you did, you are..." followed by a negative judgment is an attack, no matter how gently or intelligently spoken it is. Be clear. What are you communicating really? Do you just want to tell someone how horrible you think they are? Are you telling someone the truth or is there a deeper agenda? Are you just trying to get approval or forgiveness? Who are you communicating to and why?

Harry Truman wrote a lot of letters—so-called truthful letters when he was upset with someone. Then he threw them away. Good idea. Learning how to communicate without attack while in the midst of emotional upset takes enormous mastery. If you can wait until you are calmer, you have a better chance of communicating the truth in a way that it can be heard.

If the truth comes out, everything is possible—no matter how it may look in the moment. Sometimes, the truth seems to be written in giant, stone letters, and they land with a terrible thud. You look at this truth carved in granite and feel horrified, helpless, angry, grief-stricken, or stuck; but now it is there—not denied—and out for all to see. Sometimes there is nothing to do but walk away, continue your life, go to dinner, and go to sleep.

And then, without any effort on your part that concrete truth starts to crumble all by itself, and—lo and behold—the next time you look, the words are a little softer around the edges. And before you know it, that gigantic, immovable truth has turned into a pile of sand, something to sift through. It is very important to just let the ugly truth be, to accept and relax with it. Don't hammer at it—which actually makes it even harder. Be gentle with it. The truth has its own process.

My sister and I often referred to what we considered the magic moment in our relationship—the turn-around when we told one another the ugly truth. Throughout all our lives our relationship had been strained, to say the least. We had little in common. We often experienced hating or just simply disliking one another. I never confided in her. She never confided in me. One day we somehow ended up in a joint therapy session with my therapist and told each other the truth—not in an attacking way—just the truth. We didn't bring up the past. We didn't blame. We just told the truth about what we felt right at the moment. I remember our voices as being quiet and calm. We talked about the wall between us. We described it to one another. It was very similar: six feet thick, very high, made of brick. No climbing over it. No penetrating it. No doors through it. We acknowledged that we had kept up a pretense of being sisters when we never felt like sisters. We acknowledged that we didn't really like each other or feel we had anything in common.

We both vividly remember going to our cars afterward and waving good-bye to each other. It was a real good-bye to our relationship. We remember the relief we felt driving away. We had gotten to the bottom line. Once there, there was nothing more to say. We didn't have to lie any more.

At the end of the session nothing had shifted, nothing had changed, and I got the feeling that the therapist felt as if she had failed us. Little did she know it was just a beginning—a totally new beginning with the slate virtually wiped clean. It was the beginning of a new and real relationship. My stepfather's death a short time later brought us together again, and we began to relate to one another from a very real place.

Because it takes so much courage to tell the truth, we need to learn respect and gratitude for anyone who has the guts to tell it. We must learn to listen to the truth with compassion no matter how ugly that truth may seem. Art helps us learn that. Through art we are able to tell the terrible truth—the outrageous truth—and be applauded for it.

SUPPORT

Inherent in the principle of Communication is the concept of support. Maureen Stapleton made the audience laugh when accepting an Academy Award. She said, "I want to thank absolutely everyone I have ever known." Funny—because it was her truth.

Can you even begin to estimate how many thousands of people it took to support you to be where you are right now? Can you even begin to appreciate how many people it took to create heat, electricity, your phones, mail, clothes, food, the paint on the walls, the floor, the books, and the computer? Millions.

The stereotypical idea is that actors are difficult divas. My experience has been that successful and brilliant actors are extremely supportive and supportable people. Of course there are a few who are selfish and difficult, but the large majority of great actors are easy to work with and generous. Professional actors are willing to receive support from directors, costumers, other actors, set designers. Bad actors, or perhaps I should say inexperienced actors, are the ones who tend to be difficult.

A wonderful business slogan states *I am 100% responsible, and I cannot do it alone.* I have joked with my students that I spent much of my life doing just the opposite—not being responsible for my life and saying, "I'll do it by myself, thank you very much." I did not know what I wanted, and I did not know how to reach out for and accept support. If you don't have what you want in your life, it may be because you are not easy to support.

It is the choice to be 100% responsible that gets the champions, presidents, and stars the right to stand on the podium; but no matter how much a star seems to stand alone, no star, athlete, musician, inventor, or writer of masterpieces gets there alone. Many people helped them get there. Diana Nyad may have swum those fifty-three hours by herself from Havana to Key West, but she is the first one to acknowledge it was a team effort.

Brilliant actors are responsible. They commit to the play and the role. They show up for work on time. They are ready to work. Some actors, like Anthony Hopkins, know all their lines at the first rehearsal. I was fortunate enough to direct Joe Namath in a workshop production of Chekhov's *The Seagull*. I had somehow gotten up the nerve to ask him if he would play Dr. Dorn. I had an instinct that he would be just right to play the character who had been loved by many women.

When he committed to the role, he threw himself into it. He came to the first rehearsal with his lines learned. He came to rehearsals he didn't even need to. He listened to every direction I gave him and incorporated them into his performance beyond what I had asked. He supplied a prop that I hadn't been able to find. He grew a goatee and found his own costume. When he put it together, in spite of those stunning blue eyes, he even looked like Chekhov. No wonder the actress who played opposite him developed a wild crush on him. Friends of his who came to the play didn't recognize him at first, and then said it was the best acting he had ever done, perhaps because the role had excited him and challenged him like none other. He was the essence of The Four Principles, even if he had never heard of them.

Brilliant actors want to be surrounded by the best actors and the best directors. Without a great coach or other great athletes to learn from and be challenged by, there would be no champions. Authors need editors and readers. Presidents need campaign managers and voters. One is elected president only with massive support. We all need support that comes from above, below, and at eye level—all forms of support: Higher Powers, parents, teachers, coaches, employees, partners, employers, fans, voters, friends, mentors—even total strangers. It is essential for success. Assess for yourself if you have the kind of support you need to achieve your heart's desires. Are the people in your life hindering or helping you?

One caveat about support: be responsible. There is a difference between looking for someone to take care of you and getting appropriate support. Therapists and coaches get paid. There is mutual benefit. There are people who eagerly support others without asking for anything in return. You will and have encountered them. I have many times. That support is given freely and wholeheartedly without asking for recompense. Be careful that you are not looking for someone to take care of you, as in a "sugar daddy." The price for that kind of support is too high. Don't accept support if you suspect there is a hidden agenda and a price you might not want to pay in the future.

It is very difficult to admit that you *cannot* do it alone. But if you can fess up to that truth, you will be more amenable to finding and allowing yourself to be supported in your Commitment.

SUPPORT GROUPS

Besides having the right partner, coach, teacher, therapist, or mentor, support groups can be another way to empower your Commitments. While support groups look like a relatively modern phenomenon, even Benjamin Franklin formed his own support group for "mutual improvement." It was called the Junto and met every Friday evening. He acknowledged that this group was very important in empowering his life.

Today, for nearly every problem and issue there is a corresponding support group available. There are support groups for grief, cancer, aging—all of which can be found online. They are extremely helpful. They work. The twelve step programs brought to the world a recognition of the power of support groups.

Most of the groups available are there to help you deal with some kind of problem. But you can form your own support group to help you achieve your goals and dreams as Benjamin Franklin did. I have been involved in several support groups that I either formed or helped to form. One of my first support groups was a gathering of six women. We called ourselves "The 47th Street Flying Club" for no reason whatsoever. Our purpose was to "create viable careers in acting." It was directly out of the support of that group that I got cast in *Cloud 9* Off Broadway and won an Obie Award. They all went with me to my fourth audition for it, had breakfast with me, and met me afterward. I was so nervous and excited about the possibility of working with the director, Tommy Tune, that it was an enormous help to have them all there.

Once several of us achieved viable careers as actresses the group dissolved. The fault may have been that our purpose did not include *maintaining* viable careers. Also, several women changed their minds about their Commitment. We went our separate ways. Support groups do not have to be permanent to work.

I was in another group that started with four women and expanded to six. We called ourselves "The Rich and Famous." The name may have been frivolous, but our goals and Commitments were serious. This group went on for years. Interestingly, the one who came up with the name is what I would call rich now. She went from living in a one-bedroom apartment with four roommates to building her own multimillion-dollar home. Another of our group became a vice president of a company, making a six-figure salary. I remember one early meeting in which we talked her out of taking a job paying only five dollars an hour. "You're worth more than that!" Trembling in her boots, she turned down the job. To see her self-assurance now, compared to her insecurity then, one would not think that it was possible for a person to change and grow so much. The group stayed together for quite a long time. We became family for one another, even spending Christmases together. We went separate ways, got married, changed careers and goals, moved far apart, but we remain friends.

I now have an active writing support group. We have been meeting every week for nearly two years now. I would not have continued a very difficult project without them.

You can do anything you are deeply committed to with enough support, but you *must* get support.

Diana Nyad has this advice:

1. *We should never, ever give up!*

2. *You never are too old to chase your dreams.*

3. *It looks like a solitary sport, but it is a team effort.*

FORMING A SUPPORT GROUP

It is vitally important to the life and durability of a support group to have a stated purpose and guidelines. Otherwise, it is likely the group will crumble and dissolve. The purpose must be agreed upon equally by all members. An example of a purpose would be "to climb Mount Everest." It doesn't have to be so ambitious of course, but it must be something that you all want to do that unites you.

Some kind of structure is necessary. Decide how often you will meet and how you will conduct your meetings. The structure may be tight or loose depending upon the needs and the tastes of the people in the group. Do you create a leaderless meeting or rotate leadership? After agreeing on your Commitment, your group will need to create a structure and guidelines or rules. As I wrote previously, I prefer a kind of bowl structure rather than a rigid box—something that will allow things to happen but not limit them—some way of being together other than a "Hey-how-you-doin?" get together. Some way to focus is definitely needed. A support group should not be a party unless to have a party is the purpose of the group.

All of my support groups had stated purposes and varying guidelines that were needed in order to get through our own tendencies to fall back on our Commitments. We needed them, especially as we were confronting all the fears that came up around pursuing our dreams.

What is it you want to achieve? A support group will help speed you on your way faster than you can imagine. All it takes is at least two other people besides you. A triangle is a much sturdier shape than a straight line between two people, which can turn into a teeter-totter. Enough people to form a circle can really get things rolling. Be responsible for your Commitments and form your circle. Find a unifying purpose, create your guidelines, meet regularly, and watch how you start moving toward the fulfillment of your Commitments. Don't do it alone. Especially if your Commitments seem difficult and scary, seek all the support you can. *You cannot do it alone.*

SPEAKING AND LISTENING TO YOURSELF

You must be willing to receive support. You have to be *supportable*. You cannot be open to support if you do not have some belief in yourself and your Commitment. As a teacher, I have found it heartbreaking to hear acting students speak to and about themselves with harsh negativity. It all arises from one basic premise: "I'm not good enough." So many of them do not know how to speak or listen to themselves with compassion. They seem only to hear their own negative judgments. They can be compassionate and affirming with others, but so harsh and critical with themselves. This harsh inner voice prevents them from reaching out for support or expressing their talents in the world.

I developed *The Creative Explosion* workshops for my students largely to help them replace a dominating, negative inner voice with one that is affirming and empowering. What became glaringly clear over twenty years of workshops is that the problem lies in the relationship between the adult and the inner child. The creative inner child may have found a way to express itself in class or on stage, but in life it doesn't seem to do as well. Years ago a director frankly told me that I functioned better on stage than I did in life. He was right, and the reason was that I had not learned how to rescue and reparent my inner child yet.

Most people speak to themselves as they were spoken to, so the inner child is squelched, or rebels, or acts out. Deep down, the inner child feels unloved and unrecognized. Unfortunately, many actors had very bad or negligent parenting. A surprising number of them have had an early loss through death of a parent, so that there is a psychic chasm between their adult selves and their creative inner children. I haven't known any actors who haven't needed healing in their relationship to their own inner child. Worse, I have known many people who have no idea that such a healing is needed.

What is tragically ironic is that the more we disown our inner children, the more they run our lives and run amok. Nothing is more important in the realization of your heart's desires than the development of a compassionate and wise way of speaking and listening to yourself. The key to self-empowerment is: *Speak and listen to yourself as a loving parent would.* Do you speak and listen to yourself as a loving parent would—with respect, with compassion, without judgment, with a desire to empower with wisdom, and with patience? Do you have a healthy relationship with your inner child? If so, you have no problems with following your heart's desires and feeling your feelings. You are clear about what you want and don't want; you are alive and vibrant; your relationships are open and healthy; you make decisions easily, but not impulsively; and you are pursuing your heart's desires.

If that is not how you are, like most of us, you will need to learn to speak and listen to yourself in a new way. In Don Miguel Ruiz's wonderful book *The Four Agreements*, he speaks of being "impeccable with your word." He defines impeccable as being without sin. "Self-rejection is the biggest sin that you commit." I heartily agree. *A Course in Miracles* defines sin as error. It is simply a mistake to speak in a negative, harsh way to yourself. It doesn't help at all. To speak words is to perpetuate the thoughts behind them.

Eventually, if you do not give negative thoughts air time, or listen to them, these negative thoughts melt away. They do go away. Being impeccable in speaking to yourself requires a dedicated period of retraining the mind. I tell my students that if negative judgment did any good at all—forwarded anything at all—I would gladly use it, but that negative voice inside does not help anything, does not improve an actor's performance, and only makes it harder to relax and express openly and freely. Therefore, how you talk to yourself must *never* be negative, harsh, or critical. *Never. You must learn to talk to yourself with love, compassion, understanding, forgiveness, encouragement, approval, and inspiration—all the ways in which a loving parent would speak to you.*

What kind of communication do you listen to in your mind? Be aware. Listen to yourself. When you find yourself saying something harsh and critical, say to that voice gently and firmly, "No. I'm not going to listen to that." Then find something kind, compassionate, and validating to say instead. It takes practice and retraining.

How you speak to yourself shows up in every action. How well you take care of your body is a communication to yourself. Do you neglect taking care of yourself? Do you eat well, sleep well, take time off, and know when to urge yourself forward, know when to relax, create a safe, calm, relaxing space for yourself? Do you live in clutter and mess? What are you communicating to yourself through your environment and your relationships?

Learn to listen to what your body is saying. Pain is God yelling at us when we're not listening. Pain is resistance. If you're in emotional or physical pain, it does not mean you're bad or did something wrong. It just means you need to stop, go into it, feel it, and see what it is trying to tell you. This is not a substitute for going to the doctor or getting help. Really listening to your body may actually lead you to seek the help you need. It is difficult to go into pain—to listen to it—either physical or emotional pain—but the rewards are great if you can. So much of physical pain is stopped emotion (energy in motion). If we stop energy, there is bound to be pain. Shakti Gawain, author of *Creative Visualization*, said, "I always believe that the intensity of the whack alongside the head that life has to give us in order to get a lesson through to us is directly proportionate to the height and breadth of our stubbornness and illusion of control." In other words, if we're unwilling to listen—to hear the signals, they'll get louder in terms of pain and difficulties until we listen.

A friend was having a problem in a love relationship. In fact, there was such conflict between the two of them that on the surface there was no solution to the problem. She woke up with a terrible migraine and called me.

Of course I asked her to describe what the pain felt like.

"Like millions of people screaming at me. I can see them. They're just screaming and screaming."

"Tell them that you're willing to listen now and ask them to speak in a way that you can hear them."

After a long pause, she began to tell me what they were saying. There was remarkable wisdom in everything that was being said—far wiser than anything I could have told her. At one point her voices told her gently, "In the pain are the answers." Before she had actually experienced and been willing to listen to her pain, she had made judgments and decisions about the relationship that were not true to her heart. When she experienced her pain, she started finding her own way out of the log jam that the relationship was in.

I have experienced and observed that if we learn to really listen and pay attention to our bodies and the signals from the Universe, life may not have to be so painful. It requires listening to sensation. It requires willingness to Be Present physically, emotionally, and spiritually. No one should interpret this as if they are wrong for having pain. Not at all. There are gifts in pain if you're willing to get them. "In the pain are the answers."

If you are stopped by an inner critic, learning how to speak and listen to yourself as a loving, wise parent will empower your life more than you can imagine. However, it is a very difficult thing for so many people. The negativity sometimes seems as if it is permanently structured into the brain cells.

One of my students who is a talented composer, songwriter, and singer wrote a full-length, one-man musical based on his battle with his negative inner voices. Most of his songs were about self-hatred. Battling, conquering, getting rid of the voices is nearly impossible without going underneath them to the uncomfortable feelings in the body. That is really the battleground.

SUMMARY

Communication is the Fail Safe Principle. It is what moves things forward. Stay in communication, tell the truth, and get support. Support is key to your realizing your dreams.

THE GETTING PRESENT PROCESS

We're all just walking each other home.
—Ram Dass

I am including this exercise because it is the keystone of my workshops. It embodies and empowers The Four Principles. However, it requires a partner. Of course, it is possible to get present on your own. However, I have found that having a Compassionate Witness amps up the power of the process enormously. Because it is unlike any other technique that I have encountered, I have many partners who I have trained.

A warning: this is not a silver bullet or magic pill. Although it may completely transform you in the moment by clarifying a situation, bringing you to a higher understanding, clearing an emotion, or having a physical or emotional healing, it is like any physical exercise. It must be practiced often to effect a lasting, deep change.

It has taken me years to give this process the due respect it deserves. First emerging in classes, it expanded in my workshops, and finally became the staple that I use in my everyday life. In earlier versions of this book, the exercise was nestled into the Being

Present chapter. Now I know it requires at least a chapter, and in the future, may expand into a book of its own.

Years ago, I thought Getting Present was something one did only when deeply upset and in need of relief. Indeed, it is effective for that use. Over the years I have healed so many of the effects of my childhood traumas by going deeply into the so-called darker emotions. As a witness, I have seen how effective it is with other people suffering from post-traumatic stress disorder and depression.

Then I discovered that even when I felt calm or neutral, the process lifted me higher and surprised me with unexpected, new information and clarity. Over the years, the process has brought me into a spirituality that I had not known before. The guidance and wisdom I have received reassures me that something beyond this earthly plane exists.

When Getting Present is used repeatedly, transformation happens on what seems to be a cellular level. Patterns of responding and ways of behaving shift over time to much more positive and productive ways of being and living. The transmutations are so organic that old, automatic, negative ways of thinking disappear and are scarcely remembered. Drama and chaos fade, being replaced by peace and effectiveness. Deadness shifts to aliveness and enthusiasm. Fear is faced and walked through, enabling people to take steps toward their heart's desires. Hundreds of times I have witnessed people find healing and wisdom within themselves they never knew possible. While all that seems to promise a great deal, it is nevertheless true.

A PARTNER

During the early *Creative Explosion* workshops, I was the only one who facilitated the process. After a few years, I decided to train participants in my workshop to partner with one another, so I wrote the following guidelines. We read them. I answered any questions, and then let the participants Get Present with one another. Though I thought it risky at first, people took to it easily. I wasn't as indispensable as I thought.

With each ensuing workshop, I entrusted the process to the participants. If there were an odd number of people in the workshop, I became a partner. As a result, I, too, have had many insights and epiphanies over the years. I joked that my role had changed from facilitator to *felicitator.*

Some people, especially new people who had never been in class, were afraid to try to be Compassionate Witnesses—afraid that they wouldn't do it right. But once they did, they found it fascinating, enjoyable, and pleasing to be of help to their partners. Of course, the more one does it, the more skilled one becomes. It does not require the intense training of a therapist or psychologist. Everyone with normal intelligence and sensitivity can do it as long as they are willing to follow the guidelines of being a Compassionate Witness.

Through the Getting Present Process I have learned how true the *Course in Miracles* lesson is: "I am never upset for the reason I think." Over and over, people begin Getting Present thinking they are upset about a particular issue only to discover they are actually experiencing intense feeling about something else entirely. I cannot over-emphasize this point. Remember my friend who had just been operated on for cancer who transferred her fear into an obsession about her boyfriend? It is a clear example. But sometimes the phenomenon is much more subtle. I may be feeling a bit off and think I know the cause, only to find out when getting present what is really disturbing me.

When we can get to the real source of our upset, there is a noticeable energetic release and relief. Carl Jung said that real evil is in denial—in not confronting The Shadow—in not confronting ourselves on the deepest level. The process will certainly help you confront what is hidden from your conscious mind.

I do not claim that the process is a substitute for therapy. God knows I was blessed with an amazing shaman, fairy godmother, wise woman, compassionate, angel therapist by the name of Janice Conti. But she herself acknowledged that the Getting Present Process powerfully enhanced our work together when she told me one day that I didn't need to come back to her on a regular basis.

Part of my reluctance in writing a book about The Four Principles has been that I think readers will not practice the Process. I fervently hope you, the reader, will take the time and effort to actually try it.

Be skeptical if you wish, but as an experiment, make an earnest effort to experience the process. You will need to ask a friend to be a partner. I know that may be difficult, but remember the dictum *I cannot do it alone!* To be open and tell the truth about your bodily sensations requires trust. Choose someone you feel comfortable with and be *very* gentle when leading someone. Do not use even the subtlest form of force. If your partner is resistant, let your partner explore what resistance feels like. Perhaps the first time you attempt the process may be mainly about establishing trust. Maybe not much will happen. Be open to not much happening, and allow it. Try at least five sessions over time, over several days or weeks.

The proper support lifts us beyond our limited beliefs in our own capabilities. One person—one alone—can make the difference. In the Olympics, there is often the one person—the father, the mother, or the coach—who brought out the best in a winner. One teacher or one mentor can turn us into masters if we allow them to support us through our fear and resistance and discouragement.

One truly Compassionate Witness can help us transform our lives.

A COMPASSIONATE WITNESS

Friends may be compassionate, but they may not know how to help us get past our own minds and into our real healing and clarity. They may be very sympathetic or offer to do something to help us, but they may not know how to be a Compassionate Witness.

In order for you to do the Getting Present Process, you and your friend will need to be clear about what it means to be a Compassionate Witness. It is not difficult, but it is a special way of listening and being.

A Compassionate Witness hears us without advising.

A Compassionate Witness does not try to fix, change, heal, or alter us.

A Compassionate Witness trusts our process.

A Compassionate Witness is *unafraid of feelings.*

A Compassionate Witness is someone who will walk hand-in-hand with us through our deepest pain as we face it.

The one job for a Compassionate Witness in the Getting Present Process is to help us Be Present in our body and not let us get lost in telling stories or in describing the negative thoughts running around in our minds. That is all.

Essentially the job of the Compassionate Witness is to ask that one powerful question: *What sensation are you experiencing in your body right now?*

That is the question most of us would like to avoid because we will do almost anything we can not to feel uncomfortable sensations.

As simple as the process is, it is not easy. The tendency is for people to go back into their minds—into the story, or the obsession, rattling around on an endless wheel that gets them nowhere. The Compassionate Witness must not get caught in that wheel. The Compassionate Witness is there to help put the focus back on the body. "We can talk about that later, okay? What's going on in your body right this minute?"

You must understand that your job as Compassionate Witness is never to interfere or advise. Your job is to help your partner stay focused on the body as it connects to the imagination and Spirit.

The following are guidelines for the Getting Present Process. I do not stake a claim on the process. I consider it a gift that I was given that I pass on freely to you and anyone who wishes to use it. I have no patent on it. Here. It is yours. Please use it.

To begin, find a comfortable place where you will be uninterrupted. It is better if you can be physically together, but it is also quite effective over the phone. As the Compassionate Witness, take the time for what I call preamble, and then let people take their time *in* the process.

THE GETTING PRESENT PROCESS

Ask your partner if there is anything on which they would like to focus, such as a Commitment, a barrier, a problem, an upset, or an event. If not, it is all right if they just want clarity or direction. The following are questions you will use as a Compassionate Witness:

1. What sensation are you experiencing in your body right now?

This is the most important question to ask and one you will come back to again and again. If your partner seems to drift into thought or lack of focus, simply ask, *What is going on in your body right now?* Sometimes it is the only question you will be able to ask because your partner has difficulty experiencing sensations. Let them take their time. Don't rush. Don't push. Don't lead responses, and don't draw conclusions like "Oh, so you're really angry, aren't you?" Remember, your job is to create the space for your partner to go where they need to go and then just *follow* them where they go. Use the exact vocabulary your partner uses. If your partner answers, "I feel scared," ask, "Where in your body do you feel scared?" *not* "Where do you feel frightened?" It is very important not to add your interpretation in any way.

Validate everything. While it is important to just witness and keep your partner focused on physical sensations, you can, at times, validate what they are feeling, especially when they are going deeper or seem unable to accept what they are experiencing. You may use words or phrases like "Good" or "You're doing fine," Validate whatever a person feels or sees. If your partner says, "I feel resistance, blocked, tired, tense, stopped, or numb," you can respond, "Good. Where do you feel that?"

2. Can you go right to the center of that sensation?

Ask your partner, "Can you go right to the center of that sensation?" This question will help your partner be more specific. It may or may not elicit some resistance. It is very difficult and courageous to go to the center of sensation, but that is where healing begins. Most of us use a great deal of our energy to cling to the edges of emotional black holes without going deep into them. We think we're feeling, but we're really *fighting* feeling. When finally we surrender and go into the center of the sensation, we will find ourselves transformed and in a whole new universe.

However, if your partner shifts away from the center of a sensation, saying "It hurts!" or "It's scary!" then follow them by asking, "Where does it hurt?" or "Where does it feel scary?" Remember to use whatever vocabulary they use.

The most important part of the process is to *follow*—not to lead. Never say anything like "Go to the center of the sensation anyway." *Follow.* Your partner will know what to experience. You will not.

If they are able and willing to be in the center of a sensation, whatever it is, it may be appropriate to ask the next question:

3. What does it feel like?

Ask your partner, "What does it feel like?" This may take a moment as they search for an image or definition. This is the moment of creativity. "It feels like a knot—no, more like a bunch of knots—like a tangle—like a necklace that's got all tangled up."

Let your partner take whatever time is needed to get as specific as possible. This may or may not lead to an image. It may just remain pure sensation. That's all right. Everything is all right as long as your partner is willing to be in the experience.

All during Getting Present it may be necessary to help your partner refocus by going back to the basic question, "What sensation are you experiencing right now?"

Note: Sometimes a person may say they feel nothing. Ask them to describe what that nothing feels like or to describe any non-significant sensations, such as the feeling of clothing or the floor or the chair. Sometimes that *is* all that is going on. Being aware of small, so-called non-significant sensations *is* Being Present.

If an image does come up, ask the next question:

4. Can you see it and describe it in detail?

At this point the images may be quite ugly or frightening or distasteful, which is fine. Give your partner time to describe what is happening in detail so that it becomes real. The mind is now in collaboration *with* rather than in resistance *to* the body. In the images are the information and the healing. Images speak elegantly and eloquently. Your partner's impulse may be to get rid of the images, or to attack them, or to run from them. Encourage them to do nothing other than to just *be* with the images. If your partner can do that calmly, the next question may be:

5. In your mind's eye can you reach out and touch it gently?

This is a great question. It is the one that leads us to acceptance (Relaxation.) Because our hands are instruments of acceptance or rejection, touching something gently is a demonstration of the willingness to be with it, to acknowledge it, to connect to it. Doing this may cause some fear at first, but it is a fascinating part of the process. Even if the image is gooey, icy, fiery, violent, gross, or ugly, ask your partner if they will touch it. The results will be fascinating. A person may weep with compassion or find the thing not as difficult to touch as it first seemed. The witch that scared them at first may become enormously comforting, and they may even embrace it, or the dragon, or the ugly animal. Use your judgment. If the image is candy or food or a liquid in a vial, you may even ask your partner to taste it. If the image is lava or clouds or a magic carpet, you might ask them to touch it or lie on it.

Note: If your partner does not want to do what you suggest, do not force it. Only ask. If at any time, your partner expresses a wish to stop, let them stop. Don't say, "No, no. You're so close! Go all the way!" No matter how much you might wish it, don't do it. That means letting go of any idea you have about what the person Getting Present should be doing, thinking, or feeling.

6. What's happening now?

Once a person is well into the process, this may be the only question you need. They will know exactly how to be with the experience. Be gentle. Don't push. Let them take their time. there The person Getting Present needs time. Watch or listen to them closely. The images may change. The important thing is to let the process move where it will. Let everything be your partner's choice. Your main job is to gently, but firmly, keep them focused on their body and what arises from that connection. If your partner drifts away or becomes lost in thought, bring them back to the present with the question, "What are you experiencing in your body right now?" This basic question will get them through the process. There have been many times when I've

162

had partners say they think that they will die if they feel something. Or they say they feel dead or feel as if they are dying. Don't be afraid of such words. My response is, "Go ahead and die. It is all right. I'm right here with you." Saying that may take some courage on your part, but I have never seen anyone die in this process, even though many have been convinced they will. In fact, people are always relieved when I give them permission to die, because it is permission to feel, to really feel their real feelings. They relax, become very still, and then after some silence say how deeply peaceful they feel. Once they have permission to die, the odd thing is, they are never afraid. In fact, they may even enjoy being dead. One woman saw herself lying in a coffin strewn with petals of red roses. She liked it. People may need quite a lot of time to be dead. Let your partner take all the time they need. When people Getting Present do "come back to life" it always seems to be a rebirth experience, as if they have let go of some part of themselves that needed to be gone.

7. Do you feel present?

It is clear when this happens. The process has gone where it needs to go. The Getting Present Process may take only a few minutes, or it may last an hour or more as your partner goes through many experiences. When your partner says that they feel present, then you can go to the next important part of the process.

8. Invite your Higher Power to be with you.

Some people will say they don't believe in God or a Higher Power. That doesn't matter. It can show up as their own Wise Self. This will work just as well. Once a person is present, they have access to incredible wisdom and healing. The mind is open and ready to receive wisdom and guidance beyond what either of you knows on a conscious level. It may not be verbal. It may even be mysterious only to be understood at a later date. Or it may be very clear. The Higher Power/Higher Self may have already appeared in one form or another, or it may take a moment to show up.

Encourage the person to accept whatever shows up. The Higher Power/Higher Self takes many forms. It could be just a sense, a voice, a light. It could be a cartoon figure, a feeling, a fairy, a famous person, a friend, a family member, a beloved dog, or even their inner child. There are an infinite variety of ways in which wisdom will take shape. It truly doesn't matter whether you or the other person believes in a god or gods. Wisdom is always available when a person is fully present and able to accept where they are. At this point the process will have its own momentum that will take very little, if any, direction from you. It is often surprising, illuminating, and great fun. However, if no Higher Power/Higher Self seems to show up, let it go.

9. Do you feel complete?

A person always seems to know when a process is complete. It may not look complete to you, but stop if your partner wants to stop. If your partner feels unsatisfied, then that's where they are and need to be. *Remember that it is important only that your partner is able to be where they are—not changed or fixed.* When the process is complete, ask your partner what they got out of it. Let them share any new clarity about their Commitments and what next steps to take. Let your partner recall what happened and draw their own conclusions and lessons. Then you can add any insight you have to what your partner experienced. Your wisdom and input will be welcome *after* the process is complete.

Switch to allow your partner to lead you in the process.

Read these guidelines and put them aside. They are very specific, but do not refer to them while you are doing the process. Do not to be overwhelmed by them or dependent on them. You can read them again later. At first, all you need are the questions What sensation are you experiencing in your body right now? *And* What does it feel like? Use these and you'll be off and running.

Everyone experiences this process differently according to who they are and what they need. Some people are extremely visual; every sensation has a correlating image. Others are more emotional or direct in their experience. Some people may need more time than others. It is very individual. It doesn't matter how anyone does the process. It can be simple or complex.

Some people's emotions may shift during a session. For a long time, my processes put me in touch only with emotions that didn't change because I needed to experience and have those old, shut-down feelings. That was what I needed as I came back to life.

It's tricky. Because the process can be so powerful and so healing, people can forget its purpose. They can slip into wanting to do the process in order to shift or change what they are feeling. That's neither Being Present nor accepting being present. *The point to Being Present is to Be Present.* You have to be here first in order to take a step forward.

Of course, it is better to practice this process in a quiet, comfortable place, but that is not always possible. I have done it hundreds of times on the phone. My partners and I are so attuned to one another that we can tell by the sound of our voices when we are present. I have been able to help people as I am driving in my car without losing my attention on driving or the process. I've done it with people as they walk, ride in buses, or wait for an audition. A woman called from a diner asking for help to get present. She started out feeling very overwhelmed and tense. Her heart felt as if it were tied in taut strings. Quickly, the strings turned into violin strings on which she began playing music as her heart expanded to embrace the whole world. There was a bit of silence. I asked her, "What's happening now?"

"The waiter just brought the check." We laughed.

The process had been fast but effective. Once you are comfortable and familiar with it, you won't need to be so careful. Do it in the real world. Sometimes, there will be only time for one of you to get present. That's all right. Be committed to it, but relaxed about it.

While I have cited some examples throughout the book, here is one of my own just to solidify how it can work.

I was feeling very anxious. I had so many writing projects going, travel arrangements to make, and the house to winterize before going away to Florida and Mexico for two months. It all seemed too much. When I got present with a friend, I felt scared and tight in my heart. I saw an image of a little girl in a cabin, like in a movie. She was trying to keep the door closed against a hurricane outside. That's how I felt—like I was going to be blown away, so I was using all my strength to keep that door shut. I was present with it, so I invited my Higher Power to appear, and my Higher Power arrived on my right side as a kind of tall, male being. I couldn't really see him because I was so busy trying to keep the door closed. "Let it open," I heard.

"What?!" I thought. "I can't let the door open! I'll be blown away!" But I've gotten a little more willing over the years when my Higher Power says something, so I stepped back. The door flew open. A swift wind backed me up and then disappeared.

Outside was sunshine and a lake. Pretty, little, twittering Disney blue birds flew over the green grass and flowers. I burst into tears and understood immediately what had been making me feels so anxious: I was afraid of life being so good. In actuality, it was so good. I really had no problems. Everything was fine, and I was getting out of the cold northeast for two months of the winter. Life was very good, indeed.

The two major traumas in my life happened right in the moments when everything in my life looked very exciting and possible. The devastating events came out of nowhere without warning. That was really the bottom line for my anxiety. After Getting Present, I was calm and peaceful and able to start ticking things off my To Do list with ease.

The short process demonstrates how often we are not upset about what we think we are and what wisdom is available to us when we consciously feel and accept the sensations in our bodies. I became quite clear about the next steps to take.

The Getting Present Process puts The Four Principles together into a cohesive whole: Being Present, Relaxation, Communication, and Commitment.

The Getting Present Process will lead you to a truth and wisdom that is beyond your normal conscious state. The Getting Present Process will get you in touch with a clarity that will continue to lead you onto the next steps you need to take along the path to your heart's desires. Through the Getting Present Process you will heal your relationship to your own inner child. The Process will greatly enhance your relationship to your own body with many healing benefits physically. Ultimately, the Getting Present Process will open you to a Higher Self, a Higher Wisdom, and a Higher Power that will heal, delight, comfort, soothe, and amaze you.

If you really desire to change your life, and are willing to risk communicating, ask someone to join you in the adventure of Getting Present. It will lead you to truth, healing, clarity, and walking the path of your heart.

Remember: *As the Compassionate Witness, do not manipulate or dominate the process in any way, ever. If you never manipulate or force the process, it will always be a safe process.*

MYSTERY

*Life is a Mystery. A Mystery so awesome
that we insulate ourselves from its intensity.*
—Timothy Freke & Peter Gandy,
Jesus and the Lost Goddess

Mystery is not one of The Four Principles, but it is at the
heart and center of each of them. Mystery is what
connects them. Mystery is what surrounds them. Mystery
is the realization of them. Mystery is real. It is not some fancy
concept, but it cannot be analyzed or even understood. You cannot
make Mystery happen. You cannot force Mystery. You can only
allow Mystery. And when you are in touch with the Mystery of life,
you feel its exhilarating intensity.

In the movie *Shakespeare in Love* the visitor to the dress
rehearsal observes that the play is a mess and a disaster. Later, the
actual performance comes off swimmingly. It is a hit. "How did
that happen?" the visitor asks. The producer shrugs and says with a
smile, "It's a mystery."

I have experienced such Mystery in the realization of many
plays. At some point in rehearsal the play seems like a hopeless
mess, and then somehow—somehow—it mysteriously pulls
together, and the play works.

As actors, we work hard and in a very practical way doing our best in our roles. If we are lucky, sometimes we get cast in roles we love with the right directors and wonderful fellow actors and have experiences that take us above and beyond ourselves into Magic. Brilliant performances are mysterious and cannot be defined. They fulfill The Four Principles, and then leap into another sphere—another universe that is simply indescribable and magical.

At the heart of every great performance, the actor has a secret relationship with the character, though the actor may not be able to articulate it. Maureen Stapleton, with whom I toured in Neil Simon's *The Gingerbread Lady*, had such a connection with her character, Evy Meara. I asked Maureen about her acting technique. She said, "I learn the words and say them fast. *Fast* is good. *Faster* is better." It was all she said. In her acting she had slipped into the higher realm that was mysterious even to her.

Anthony Hopkins said that he prepares for a role by learning the words so well that they are automatic, and he doesn't have to think about them. He always seems to have a secret when he acts, one that he particularly enjoys, as in his terrifying and brilliant performances as Hannibal Lecter.

It is possible to stumble upon this kind of elevated creative expression, but usually it is only after years of experience that one can achieve such mastery and experience Mystery. As with meditation or art, it takes decades of practice.

The more you immerse yourself in The Four Principles, the more you realize how intertwined and connected they are. Each seems 100% important, yet all are interdependent and work together. Because of their interdependence, it is almost impossible to focus on one without including the others. One can separate the four elements fire, water, air, earth; but how can one talk about fire without acknowledging the products of earth that are needed to create fire—wood or coal? How can one speak of fire without acknowledging the air it needs in order to burn? How can one speak of air without noticing the clouds of vapor? Yes, they can be listed separately, but they do not exist separately.

In fact, the four elements are nice parallels to The Four Principles. I would equate Being Present to earth, water to Relaxation, fire to Commitment, and air to Communication.

THE ROCKET

Let's assume this *is* rocket science for a moment. You are the captain. Where do you want to go? What is your Commitment? In this analogy Commitment comes first. You point to the heavens, and you say, "I want to go to that star." Or, you just may want to go out and explore open space.

What do you do then? Start communicating. Communication is the fuel that moves things forward. You get your support team. You order gas. A lot of Communication is needed to get your rocket off the ground—along with the passion of your Commitment.

It is good to be hyped, inspired, and enthusiastic, but you must communicate no matter how you feel. Passion may provide the energy to start communicating, but passion alone is not what gets you there. You may lose touch with your passion and inspiration many times along the way. That is why it is important to remember that Communication is what will get you there. Communication is your fuel.

Every pilot knows that no rocket's trajectory is a straight line. In fact, rockets always go off course. You can count on it. In a rocket's journey, the computers tracking its path are always assessing where the rocket is and making constant course corrections. In other words, the rocket needs to Be Present in order to get to its destination. A rocket needs to be constantly in Communication with itself in order to stay on or get back on track.

You need to constantly assess where you are. "I'm tired. I need to take a five-minute break." "Ooops. I'm going in the wrong direction. I need to get clear about where I am going."

And Relaxation? I have heard it said that velocity is power. If so, what creates the potential for the greatest velocity? Space.

How much energy it takes to lift up out of gravity—literally and figuratively—attaching seriousness, importance, significance, fear of success or failure make it very difficult to move through space. The heavier we are, the harder it is.

We need to do whatever we can to lighten up. We need to eliminate the unnecessary baggage of struggle and negative judgment and comparison thoughts like "My rocket's not as big as his"; "My rocket's not as thin as hers"; "She's going to Venus. I should be going to Venus, too." We need to throw out the old ideas, contexts, beliefs, and ways of thinking that make it so difficult to get our rockets off the ground. It will take some time. We need to go through stages of letting go of our past.

Once we have let go of gravity and resistance, it is possible to travel at light speed. Relaxation is vital to getting to your destination and having fun on the journey.

Besides, what's the point of achieving your goals if you didn't enjoy the trip? And to be really relaxed, I personally make sure I have a good Co-Pilot.

All the principles work together and are needed to get your rocket to your heart's desires. This may be a rather simplistic analogy, but it does illustrate how all Four Principles work together to achieve any Commitment.

MYSTERY/THE ULTIMATE OF THE FOUR PRINCIPLES

The more fully you actualize the Four Principles the more you will experience them leading from the practical to the mysterious:

Being Present

When you are truly present, you are in "the power of now," as Eckhart Tolle describes it in his book of the same title. Being here now has been the aim of mystics for eons. The closer you get to Being Present, the closer you get to God's self-description: I AM.

When you learn how to be with and listen to your body, you are able to access a level of inner wisdom that is profound. Joan Didion wrote about her migraine headaches, "And once it comes, now that I am wise in its ways, I no longer fight it. I lie down and let it happen. At first every small apprehension is magnified, every anxiety a pounding terror. Then the pain comes, and I concentrate only on that. Right there is the usefulness of migraine, there in that imposed yoga, the concentration on the pain. For when the pain recedes, ten or twelve hours later, everything goes with it, all the hidden resentments, all the vain anxieties. The migraine has acted as a circuit breaker, and the fuses have emerged intact. There is a pleasant convalescent euphoria. I open the windows and feel the air, eat gratefully, sleep well. I notice the particular nature of a flower in a glass on the stair landing. I count my blessings."

Mystics have used self-inflicted pain as a way of elevating themselves into a spiritual state. I'm not recommending pain any more than I would recommend seeking only pleasure to reach enlightenment. We encounter enough pain and pleasure in the process of living. Be present with whatever is here right now, right now, right now. This will put you on your path of enlightenment more surely than you can imagine.

With experience at Being Present, you will no longer be so afraid of the darker emotions. Yes, darker emotions are uncomfortable, but with help you can accept them and be kinder and more compassionate to yourself when you are ill, in pain, depressed, exhausted, angry, or in despair. You can work through your tendencies to isolate and instead, reach out for help. You can ride out the dark nights of the soul, and believe reassurances that you will get through it and that you will be stronger for it. You can develop the courage to feel, even when you think it will kill you. For me, Getting Present is magical and can connect me with Mystery no matter what I am feeling. The key word in the process is *compassion*. When we can feel and achieve *true compassion* for ourselves and others no matter what we and they are feeling, we are in the loving arms of Mystery. I Am is God.

Relaxation

Method actors strive for what is known as *moment-by-moment acting*, but the term conjures up a kind of jerky movement in my mind. What *moment-by-moment acting* really means is being in an energetic flow of Being Present and Communicating truthfully with such immediacy that there is no thinking about it. It is like riding on a magic carpet. There is no mistaking it.

There is an energetic current in life. When you are able to practice no force and no resistance and get into the flow, you know it. You know when to move, when to rest, when to eat, when to take action, and literally how to go with the flow.

Of course, you will sometimes move out of the current of your life. When that happens, Getting Present will carry you back into the current.

When we actors learn to let go of trying to control our performances, let go of our ideas about what they should look like, and surrender to the energetic flow, we realize our roles better than we thought possible. Our performances surprise us and carry us.

Creativity is like that. So it is with life.

When you let go of your ideas of how it should be—not let go of what you want, but what form it should take—when you let go of your will and let your heart and life lead, then you find yourself flowing in the space of Magic and Mystery.

When you accept where you are and trust the future, you begin to see the flow of your life as a wonderful creation. To choose to operate and act from faith rather than fear is an act of bravery, going against the worry that tells you everything is dangerous, you better cover your ass, grab what you can, and always be on the defensive.

Faith does not require a religion. Faith can be the belief that there is a way, and things will work out if you are patient and proceed with calm. Fear urges you to do things not in alignment with your heart and harmful to you and to others.

Fear is loud. Faith is quiet.

It is challenging not to act from fear and all the temptations that fear presents. The more you *choose* faith, the more you challenge your own negative beliefs and, instead, choose to accept and trust, the more your experience will corroborate this choice. When you move through scary situations with faith, you will find yourself in touch with the compassionate energy of Mystery.

Wise beings are unafraid of life. And that state of mind is achieved by choosing to accept and trust moment by moment in the flow of everyday life.

Communication

The more in Communication you are with yourself, with others, and with your own intuition, the more you discover that *We Are One* is not merely a nice thought, some jingle for a telephone company or a song for a group of famous singers. In the Newtonian world there is separation. Likewise, in our trained experience we see ourselves as separate from it all. Everything wrong is out there. The world is composed of ourselves encased in our skin, and everything else is outside us.

However, in the world of quantum physics everything is interrelated and causes scientists to create various, mind-expanding theories to explain it. Just the recognition that we are in a constant interchange with the world through the most basic means of breath belies how separate we are from everything around us When we reach the ultimate of Communication, we begin to experience inexplicable connectedness as if we are electrons mysteriously communicating across space and time..

I have observed that when we can consciously and authentically change our spin on something, it affects those who were involved in the old spin telepathically, automatically, and with faster-than-light speed. Have you ever had the experience of owning your part in the upset in a relationship, felt an internal shift, only to discover that the other person who was involved had made a corresponding shift? Your internal shift has to be real. This means letting go of blaming the other person or identifying them in a certain light. It probably involves understanding that your emotional upset is a reflection of a much earlier pain in your life.

When you shift away from the present difficulty and realize a pattern connected to an earlier pain, it does not mean that your relationship will become what you want it to be—what your will is attached to it being—but it does mean a relaxation of your will, which will allow the relationship to be what it is. The truth will either set you free of the relationship, or else set you free in it. When you truly shift, the world around you shifts. It does. Life is an inside job.

One theory to explain this phenomenon is seeing the Universe as a Hologram. [See *The Holographic Universe* by Michael Talbot.] If so, the tiniest change in an atom affects the entire Universe. If so, one person is the holographic reflection of the entire Universe. This idea is mind-boggling but agreed upon by most mystics and by some highly educated, respected, and intelligent scientists alike. It is an idea that's fairly indigestible in the mundane world.

It has been theorized that the myriad of subatomic particles being identified don't actually exist until they are seen by someone. Weird as that possibility is, I have seen the evidence of it in life— that something does not truly exist until it is witnessed. Over and over again in my classes, as soon as I see some trait of a student that he or she has not recognized, it becomes real. Sometimes the attribute while disguised seems to be a problem. However, when it is identified without judgment, it becomes a virtue. Once something is seen, it does not get unseen. Instead, it becomes real.

We communicate energetically. I was partnering with someone in a workshop, sitting on the floor comfortably as she sat on a couch. When it was my turn to Get Present, I felt good, really good.

The feeling increased. I started feeling ecstatic in my heart and torso. I saw an image of a golden spiral in the center of my body. Coming from the inside of the spiral were glittering, pink explosions like gentle fireworks of varying shades from light pink to magenta. The image was beautiful, and it felt both wildly exciting and calming at the same time. I had never felt anything like it. It felt sacred: female, active, and creative. I identified it as Goddess Energy. God had always been masculine to me. This was distinctly different.

As I described it and felt it, it seemed to fill the room. I noticed that my partner seemed to be feeling it, too. We looked at one another and started laughing at the sheer ecstasy of it, as if the communication of the energy was actually increasing it.

In another workshop, a woman began to feel a very powerful energy in her body that at first was overwhelming to her. She was struggling with it, so I asked her to look someone in the eyes and share it with the person. She turned to a woman sitting close by. Soon the other woman became excited and high on this woman's energy. They were giggling and laughing and highly entertaining to the rest of us as they shared this energy. Everyone in the workshop was affected by it. It was very similar to what happened to my partner and me when I experienced the Goddess Energy.

In one ten-minute silence that is part of *The Creative Explosion* workshop, someone started laughing. She felt it was inappropriate and struggled to stop. I encouraged her, "It is all right. Go ahead and laugh." She did. It was so infectious that we all laughed wildly for the full ten minutes. It was very refreshing, and it reminded me of the time I had started laughing while waiting in a room of extras during the filming of *Suspect*, and they all laughed, too.

After the close of the workshop that night, a few of us watched a documentary that I had selected randomly at the library. Astoundingly, it was about laughing clubs, people who get together and laugh for no reason. They call it laughing yoga. We had no idea such a thing existed. It was one of those synchronistic experiences that would have delighted Carl Jung.

When you experience and own the sensations of love, bliss, ecstasy, joy, excitement, and peace, that energy will be contagious to everyone around you. They will feel this energy. You will enliven and enlighten everyone you contact.

Conversely, when you *consciously* own the sensations around the so-called darker emotions of anger, hatred, sadness, fear, despair, and depression, no one will be negatively affected by your feelings. In fact, you will relieve everyone you contact. Every time I have been the witness for someone who is experiencing and accepting intense emotions like rage, hatred, sadness, despair, fear, depression, I have not been affected adversely in any way by their feelings. I have always experienced relief.

Commitment

The more fearlessly committed you are to your authentic path, the more magical your journey will be. All sorts of unexpected gifts will show up to surprise and delight you. The greater the love, the greater the Commitment. Doing what you love, following the path with love is the advice of the wisest people. It does take courage. It means saying NO to what is not your path. It means saying NO to your shoulds and oughtas. It means saying NO to the fears that drag you backward. When you have the courage to step onto the path, leaving behind all your considerations and looking ahead with Relaxation and trust, the Universe will support you in ways that will seem magical.

It does not matter what you are committed to, as long as it connects to your heart. A great Commitment is expansive and includes other people. A great Commitment is a vision set in love. A playwright writes a play. A producer or a director falls in love with it and takes responsibility for realizing it. He holds the vision and enrolls other people into a production team—investors, actors, designers, publicists. I have been so lucky to work with great teams on realizing the vision of a play or a movie, and it is thrilling, being part of a vision as it is realized is deeply satisfying.

I recently went to a memorial celebration of a woman who had lived her vision for more than thirty years. She was the managing director of The Dolphin Research Center in Grassy Key, Florida. Along with her husband, she had been driven by her love of dolphins to create a safe, loving haven for them there. Her heartfelt Commitment enrolled others, including a daughter who is a trainer at the Center and many of the staff who have also been there from the time of its meager beginnings in the eighties. More than two hundred people gathered to honor this woman who held the vision, kept her Commitment, and fiercely fought for the preservation and safety of marine life and the environment. It was all founded in love—of the dolphins, her family, and the people she worked with. If you want Magic in your life, create or align yourself with a vision that speaks to your heart.

Remember that Commitment is founded in knowing the truth about what you need and want. It does not have to be grandiose. It can be very simple. It just has to be the truth. One time years ago, I was headed for an acting class in New York City. It was a cold, rainy day. The neighborhood was ugly. All I saw was ugliness. I was depressed and very unhappy. I didn't fight it. I heard a kind of voice asking, 'What would make you feel better right this minute—right this second?"

"Maybe a beautiful flower," I thought.

Almost the moment that thought crossed my mind, a man leaning against a building said to me, "You look like you could use a flower." That stopped me dead in my tracks. I just gawked at him too stunned to respond. He walked into the building he had been leaning against. I didn't move. He came out and handed me more than a flower, he gave me an armful of roses. I swear.

I don't remember what I said to him. I think I told him that I had just wished for a flower. I didn't ask his name. He didn't ask mine.

I walked on to the acting class, went in, and told the story. I remember thinking that what happened had been a stunning anomaly, a crack in the Universe, something that was incredibly unusual. I have since observed that those kinds of things actually happen frequently when and if—and this is a big one—*when* and *if* we are *truly* Present and clear about what we want and need *in the moment*. It is *all* in the moment.

Another time, I was told something by a friend that caused me incredible heartache. I prayed, "God, help me out here. I'm in terrible pain." That was all I could pray. The doorbell rang. That in itself was highly unusual at my house in the country. I went to the front door. A kid was selling something. He was sweet and playful, and we ended up singing a song together. It lightened my heart immediately. I didn't win the lottery. I didn't get a vacation. I got help in the moment. It was enough.

Eckhart Tolle wrote, "What you need will show up the moment you need it—not a moment before and not a moment after." I could name many times when something I really needed showed up at the moment I needed it. One night during a class, I mused about hanging a lovely hammock I bought in my living room. A young man who just happened to have been visiting the class came by the next day with two large hooks and put them in supporting posts in a jiffy. I hung the hammock between them. I never saw him again, but I've used the hammock for years.

One day I was sitting on my deck and noticed a clump of bamboo in my enormous bamboo grove growing too close to the house. I wanted to get rid of the clump, but I knew it would be too hard physically for me to do.

That evening I was washing dishes and was again surprised by someone knocking on my front door. It was a man from a tree company. He asked if it would be all right if he cut down some bamboo for his use. "Sure," I wiped my hands on my towel and pointed, "how about that clump right there."

"Perfect," he said. I finished my dishes and looked outside. The clump was gone.

These are small examples. I could cite many more. I have experienced it so often that my belief that what I need will show up when I need it has been reinforced often. It certainly enhances my relaxation and calms any tendency to worry about the future. Is it true? Well, it has been true for all the past years of my life. Why should it change? Have I always gotten what I wanted? No. Have I gotten everything that I have needed? Yes. I choose to believe that will continue throughout the rest of my life.

Magic is real. It does not only happen in great enterprises. It exists in every moment of life. The rarity of experiencing Magic is only because we are not present enough to see it. We move through life worrying about the future, thinking about the next moment, the next activity, what we're going to have for lunch, how we're going to make something work or happen, and we totally miss the Magic moments.

ECSTASY AND MYSTERY

In class I once wondered aloud why so many people seem to resist or fear happiness. A student responded, "Because we are not programmed for ecstasy." We all laughed because it resonated as the truth.

A woman in a *Creative Explosion* workshop was Getting Present around the problem she had getting herself out into the world as an actress. She is a wonderful actress. Her acting is not and never has been the problem. It is her fear of making phone calls and going to auditions that is the problem. When she got Present, she felt overwhelmed and weighted down by the thought of making phone calls. The idea of putting herself out into the world made her feel like Sisyphus pushing a boulder up a mountain. Struggling with the boulder was exhausting to her.

The image was very clear, so I asked her to just touch the boulder instead of trying to push it. She did. "What does it feel like?" I asked her. Her answer surprised her. "It is still!" I wasn't sure what was interesting about that until she explained that when she stopped pushing, she noticed that it didn't roll back on her.

Then she said, "It is not as big as I thought. I'm taller than it." I love this part of the process—watching the transformation happen with no interference or effort on my part. I love the surprise and wisdom of it. She started to laugh with genuine amusement. "What?" I asked, wanting in on the joke.

"Well, I can see myself with this boulder. It is now in a field—a big field. There's plenty of space around it. I *could* just stop pushing it and walk around it, but for some reason, I thought I had to push this boulder across the field!" We laugh together. This is the essence of enlightenment for me—to literally lighten up and to laugh about the barriers we create and how we punish ourselves—like Robert De Niro's character in *The Mission*, who in a form of penance drags a bag of heavy, useless stuff up a mountain. The more enlightened natives do him a favor: they cut the rope. His baggage tumbles down the mountain, and they laugh.

My workshop participant now understands that in some way the boulder has been protective. It has kept her from walking across the field to what she wants. She is in a state of wonder at this self-discovery. It is completely new information—an astounding idea.

She feels much lighter in her body having gotten the information it was trying to tell her. The field in her mind is still vivid. It is so vivid that I can see it, too. She describes other boulders lying in the field and how silly she has been to go from boulder to boulder without just walking around them. I posit the possibility that what she has really been afraid of is not failure—not rejection—but happiness and success—that *that* was why she had stopped acting because she was just beginning to experience success. She looks at me wide-eyed. She gets it. Yes, she did quit acting, not because she was failing at it, but because she had been actually succeeding at it and lying to herself that she was failing.

The Gate to Heaven is guarded by demons that will try to stop you from entering. Thank them. Be grateful for them. Every one you wrestle with strengthens you and makes it possible for you to be strong enough for the ecstasy of Mystery. One might say that life is a training for ecstasy. We must be terribly strong and vulnerable, wide-awake, and relaxed in order to withstand that kind of vibration, that kind of light. Why are we working so hard to root out the dark places? It is so we can bear bliss, so we can bear loving in that open-hearted way.

The Energy of Mystery can have enormous power. One could call it Cosmic Creative Energy. Being in touch with Cosmic Creative Energy can be scary because it is huge. It requires you to expand beyond your identification of yourself. It requires you to let go of every lousy idea you have about yourself and life. The energy *is* too much for us to hold alone. We must share it. The more we have, the more this energy needs to be given away. Fear is contracting. Love is expanding. Expansion rather than contraction is what Mystery is about.

People who have chosen expansion rather than fear and contraction are shining examples in the world. Paul Newman expanded his mastery of the energy flow with all his work with children, along with his wife, Joanne Woodward. Steven Spielberg uses his power expansively. There is a gentleness and quietness about these people that includes humility. Humility is an attribute of someone who has stepped into Mystery and is flowing with it. Oprah Winfrey, among others, remains a human being in spite of her power. Hers is an expansive use of Creative Energy. Many of the people who use this energy to help others are working quietly in the world without a lot of hoopla and publicity.

If we're not really present, we can actually prefer poor imitations of heaven. We want ecstasy, but instead of strengthening ourselves to be able to withstand it, we turn to addictions. There are those who talk a great deal about being in touch with Love and the Mystery of life, but their lives don't actually work. They float around in an airy-fairy land without really being responsible for their lives, maybe high on drugs. Talk is not it. We can't skip over the tough stuff. We have to get in there with reality before we can get to the real Magic.

Sometimes people can step into Cosmic Creative Energy before they are really masterful enough to manage it—like lottery winners whose lives are ruined because they cannot handle such financial windfalls. Gurus have delivered something called *shaktipat* to devotees who then have psychotic breaks. If Mystery is not held by people in touch with faith and love, it is dangerous for them and others.

However, if you apply the very practical Four Principles, you will go no faster than you can bear. When you own your fear and hatred and do not project them onto others, you will be safe. When your Commitments are connected to your heart, you will be safe. When you stop trying to control yourself and others, you will be safe. When you choose Love, you will be safe.

To those of you who feel your life is about as far from Mystery and Magic as you can get, let me take your hand and say I understand. Let me reassure you that you can step into that magical flow in an instant if you will be present, accept where you are, and trust the future.

To those of you who have been skating along only to find the magical ice is no longer under your feet and you are stumbling across dirt, if you fall on your face, get up and dust yourself off, as the song says, and keep going. There is more ice to skate on ahead.

To those of you who don't believe in Mystery, this will all sound like gobbledygook and insanity. That's okay. Just commit to The Four Principles. They work. They put your tires on the road and will getcha where you want to go.

In the movie *American Beauty*, Kevin Spacey's character says as he dies, "Sometimes I feel like I'm seeing it all at once, and it is too much. My heart fills up like a balloon that's about to burst, and then I remember to relax and stop trying to hold onto it. And then it flows through me like rain. And I can't feel anything but gratitude for every single moment of my stupid, little life. You have no idea what I'm talking about, I'm sure. But don't worry. You will some day."

MYSTERIOUS *AND* WONDERFUL

One very cold January night, I was driving home after seeing some students perform beautifully. I was grateful and happy and felt deeply at peace. I glanced at the digital clock in my car. It read 11:11. "Odd," I thought. I had been glancing at clocks a lot lately just at 11:11. "I wonder what that means?"

At that moment I heard a voice say, "Katherine. Life is more mysterious and wonderful than you can imagine." The voice, sounding something like my own, did not startle me. Yet, it really didn't feel as if I was *thinking* the thought. It felt as if it was being told to me.

The voice repeated the sentence gently and compassionately. "Katherine. Life is more mysterious and wonderful than you can imagine."

"Mysterious," I could agree with, but I was less sure about categorizing life as "wonderful."

As I drove, the voice repeated the sentence over and over with a kind of quiet intensity as if something or someone was speaking to me and really wanted me to know it. "Katherine. Life is more mysterious and wonderful than you can imagine." I laughed out loud as I parked my car in my barn. The voice stopped. It was 11:12. I joked with myself. "Wow, I'm turning into Shirley MacLaine."

Cynicism aside, as I walked up to my house, I felt deeply reassured. I stopped and looked up. At that moment seeing the full moon in the sky, I did get it. Life really is more mysterious and wonderful than I had ever imagined. I could almost hear Jeannette MacDonald and Nelson Eddy singing, *"Ah! Sweet mystery of life at last I've found you!"*

After that, my eyes kept being drawn to clocks exactly at 11:11 A.M. or P.M. At night sometimes I would be sound asleep and simply open my eyes and see 11:11 on the digital clock next to my bed. Every time I saw that number I was reminded that life is more mysterious and wonderful than I can imagine.

I noticed that the four ones seemed to symbolize The Four Principles and were connected by two dots of—well, Mystery. If you look at The Four Principles in this 11:11 configuration, they are balanced. On the one side is Female and on the other Male. Being Present and Relaxation seem to me to be female principles—inward and receiving—and Commitment and Communication have male energy—outward and toward action. Take a moment to see how balanced you are in that regard. Are you more adept at Being Present and Relaxation, or at Commitment and Communication?

Glancing at clocks at 11:11 happened so frequently that I wrote a post about it on my web site. Someone emailed me writing that seeing clocks at 11:11 is a wide-spread phenomenon. She suggested I Google 11:11. Indeed, there were many web sites and postings by people who found themselves glancing at clocks precisely at 11:11. Every time I do it now, I use it as an opportunity to take a moment to be grateful for all that I have—for the sweet Mystery of Life.

When you are deeply committed, when you are present, when you relax and connect to the oneness of life, you will experience Mystery. You will know moments of serendipity, synchronicity, and Magic beyond the normal experience of everyday life. You will find your life to be more mysterious *and* wonderful than you can possibly imagine.

ACKNOWLEDGMENTS

I want to thank the people who have come to my classes over the years. I can list only the people for whom I have email addresses, so I apologize to the many other students and *Creative Explosion* participants whose names are not here. Every single one of you has contributed to my education as a teacher and a person. Thank you. Amy Andrews, James Babbin, Kurt Bardele, Carol Birch, Paul Bodden, Mark Bogosian, Betsy Bowen, Anne Brady, Lynn Braz, Sheri Bresson, Michele Broder, Bill Broderick, David Brooks, Gary Matthew Binnie, Anne-Marie Brule, Phillip Burrill, Anthony Ciccotelli, Routh Chadwick, Sarah Dacey-Charles, Kathy Cokkinos, Deborah Connelly, Cathy Cross, Marilyn Despres, Ellie Devers, Leslie Diamond, Henri Douvry, Elly-Anne Ehrman, Marcia Ellis, Elaine Evans, Cheryl Fields, Mary Finnegan, Edmound Fitzpatrick, Alexandra Frederick, Rodney Freeze, Ellie Fordyce, Deanna Fraschilla, Rob Gardner, Greg Gasawski, Kate Goehring, Gail Goldberg, Eric Scott Gould, Ann Gulian, Katherine Gray, Judith Greentree, Angelo Gugglielmo, Michael Habetz, James Hallett, Art Hansen, Ian Hersey, Eve Holbrook, Connie Illowitz, Melissa Kalt, Geraldine Kennon, Kathy Kiley, John Kochiss, Serafim Kotsogiannis, Antoinette LaVecchia, Robyn Lee, Brian Loeffler, Jennifer Lickson, Richard Luciano, James Luce, Maggie Maes, Kate Mailer, Patrice Maltas, Julie Manon, Richard Marshall, Vanessa Maruskin, Deb Mathews, Jen Scott Mobley, Carla Mason Ness, Brian Olivieri, Kim O'Halloran, Joanne Parady, Aileen Pare, Nancy Pasquariello, Rhiannon Perry, Dael Piro, Ross Pivec, Jeffrey Polsky, Jonathan Prager, Phil Rafferty, Mark Ransom, Sarah Rice, Eric Roffman, Gloria Rosen, Vipin Sharma, Michael Shepley, Suzanne Sheridan, Katherine Silvan, Cecilia Soprano, Stacie Teele,

Marcia Tippit, Brian Tracy, Maureen Tracy, Judith Van Buren, Vickie Varnuska, Dan Verrichione, Susan Barnes Walker, Sheri Wicks, Brooks Willich, Debra Wiley, Babs Winn, Myrton Running Wolf, and Tina Zaremba. I also add thanks to Art Hanson for his work on the earlier versions of this book.

Many thanks to Bill Broderick, and Tom Connor for their expert help in editing and friendship. Jeffrey Polsky stepped way beyond friendship's call to edit not only one but two versions of this book. Thanks, too, to Ellie Devers for months of fascination and a lot of laughter as we partnered in the Getting Present Process, and to Patrice Maltas for her friendship and Commitment to The Four Principles. I thank my dear friends and long-time support-group members who have helped me over so many obstacles over the years, held my hand, encouraged me, cried with me, and laughed with me: Julie Janney, Madalasa Mobili, Sarah B. Prediger, Gale Ricketts, Linda Howard, Liz Morten, and especially Martha Rhodes, who has been an enormous help in transforming these pages into an actual book.

I thank my sister, Eloise Kerr, for her constant support and the love we shared. Thanks to James J. Mapes for his unwavering support and friendship over the years, as well as Susan Granger for her creative support and a piña colada when I really needed it. Thanks too, to Linda Wechter for taking care of too many things to mention.

I give loving thanks to and for my shaman therapist healer, Janice Conti, who has gone to the darkest places in my soul with me and shed light on them all with such deep compassion and laughter.

My deep thanks to some special teacher/directors: June Havoc, Tommy Tune, Mike Nichols, Michael Howard, Ron Lagomarsino, Michael Mayer, and Marsha Mason. Thanks to Christopher Durang for the great gift of *Laughing Wild* and our special friendship over the years, and to his wonderful husband, John Augustine, who has become a cherished friend.

I also want to thank everyone in the Theatre Artists Workshop of Norwalk, Connecticut. As a member of this group of professional actors, writers, and directors for more than thirty years, I am deeply grateful for the constant inspiration of their work and for the space they have provided for me to stretch as an actress, rewrite as a writer, explore as a director, and have so much fun. See you at Penny's Diner after.

INDEX

E. KATHERINE KERR is an actress, writer, teacher, director, and workshop leader. She won an Obie Award, a *Villager* citation, and a Drama Desk nomination for her portrayals of three characters in *Cloud 9*. A second Drama Desk nomination followed for her portrayals of the woman in Christopher Durang's *Laughing Wild*. Her featured roles in films include Harriet Tollman in *Songcatcher*, the Attorney General in *The Siege*, Congresswoman Grace Comisky in *Suspect*, and Gilda Schultz in *Silkwood*. She is also featured in *Next Stop Wonderland*, *The Imposters*, *The Devil's Advocate*, *Power*, and *Children of a Lesser God*. Her television credits include many appearances on *Law and Order*, recurring roles on *The Guiding Light*, *One Life to Live*, and *All My Children*, as well as the BBC production of *The Buccaneers*.

On Broadway, she appeared opposite Frank Langella in *Passion*, *No Place to be Somebody*, and *Night Watch*. She played Tess in Keith Bunin's *The Credeaux Canvas*, and two characters who argue with each other in *She Stoops to Comedy* both at Playwrights Horizons. Her own play *Juno's Swans*, a comedy about sisters produced in New York City at Second Stage Theatre, was sold-out and held-over. ABC commissioned a television pilot that she wrote based on the play. Her one-woman show *On the Zip-Line* was performed at the Theatre Artists Workshop in Connecticut, at the Harold Clurman Theatre in New York City, and at Queen's College in Canada. Her play *Intelejunt Dezyne* was presented as a benefit at T.A.W., and produced at Fairfield Theatre. A third play, *The Edge of Chaos*, has been in development at T.A.W. She also directed *The Seagull* and appeared as Arkadina, with Joe Namath as a memorable Dorn, at the Arclight Theatre.

Kerr has taught acting at Sarah Lawrence College, Yale University, New York University Tisch School of the Arts Playwrights Horizons Theatre School, the 42nd Street Collective, and privately for the past twenty-five years. Expanding on the Four Principles that she developed as she taught acting, Kerr originated *The Creative Explosion*, a two-day workshop that applies the same principles to creativity and life. The workshop has been ongoing four to five times a year in Connecticut for the last twenty years. She has also conducted the powerful workshop with the skillful co-leadership of dolphins at the Dolphin Research Center in Marathon Key, Florida. As an author, her work includes a book for actors, *The Four Keys to Authentic Acting*, and her autobiography, *How I Became a Not Famous Actress and Survived*.

Her web sites are EKatherineKerr.com and TheFourPrinciples.com.

On E. Katherine Kerr and The Four Principles

Katherine's courageous ability to live utterly in the moment is what she brings to teaching and what she teaches. She refers to it as "brilliant acting," but it seems to me to be more "brilliant living"—a quality that causes a specific few to shine in a field of many...Her methods move the actor forward with each encounter, but the principles themselves can be employed to move an artist forward for a lifetime.

—Jean Dobie Giebel, professor,
Department of Drama and Dance, Hofstra University

I was in a production of *Urban Blight* at the Manhattan Theatre Club in New York City with E. Katherine Kerr. I watched her, riveted in the wings every night, in one of the most powerful moments I had ever seen on stage yet it was never the quite the same. Always deeply affecting, her emotion seemed to burst forth fresh and different every night while always real and truthful. I thought, "Secretly within me I know I have the ability to do that. I want to know how. I want to know how to do that." I knew I was in the presence of someone who held the answers. My inner voice was telling me this was my next guru. When she told me about her *Creative Explosion* workshop; a weekend of intense training, exercises, and information applying her Four Principles to acting and to life, I quickly enrolled. It was in that powerful workshop that I finally found out how to be fully present on stage. My eight shows a week have never been the same. While the workshop had an enormous effect on my acting, unexpectedly, it also touched me more deeply. It was life-changing. The Four Principles are life-altering. I can't shout it from the rafters loudly enough or enough times. Do yourself a favor and read this book.

—Faith Prince,
Tony Award-winning actress

"E. Katherine Kerr is a brilliant actress. It is not surprising that her method of teaching acting is as alive and plugged into human behavior as are her portrayals of characters you would swear have just been brought into the room from their real lives. It is very rare to find a great teacher of acting who both has the gift and the craft to be able to pass it on."

—Mike Nichols,
Emmy, Grammy, Oscar and Tony (EGOT)
Award-winning director, producer, and performer

31713029R00124

Made in the USA
Middletown, DE
09 May 2016